**THE ROYAL COURT
THEATRE PRESENTS**

VIOLENCE AND SON

By GARY OWEN

Violence and Son was first performed at the Royal Court Jerwood Theatre Upstairs, Sloane Square, on Wednesday 3rd June 2015.

VIOLENCE AND SON
BY GARY OWEN

CAST (in alphabetical order)

Jen **Morfydd Clark**
Rick **Jason Hughes**
Liam **David Moorst**
Suze **Siwan Morris**

Director **Hamish Pirie**
Designer **Cai Dyfan**
Lighting Designer **Lizzie Powell**
Composer & Sound Designer **Mark Melville**
Assistant Director **Roy Alexander Weise**
Casting Directors **Amy Ball & Louis Hammond**
Production Manager **Jessica Harwood**
Fight Director **Bret Yount**
Costume Supervisor **Holly White**
Stage Managers **Jules Richardson, Kate Wilson**
Stage Management Work Placement **Oana Birgean**
Set constructed by **Ridiculous Solutions**
Scenic Artist **Sarah Hall**

The Royal Court and Stage Management wish to thank the following for their help with this production:
Jonathan Asser, Trisha Christie-Kelly at Barnardos.

VIOLENCE AND SON
THE COMPANY

Gary Owen (Writer)

Theatre includes: **We That Are Left, Mrs Reynolds & the Ruffian, Perfect Match** (Watford Palace); **Iphigenia in Splott** (Sherman Cymru); **Love Steals Us from Loneliness** (National Theatre Wales/ Sherman Cymru), **Free Folk** (Forest Forge), **The Shadow of a Boy** (National); **Crazy Gary's Mobile Disco** (Paines Plough/Sgript Cymru); **The Drowned World** (Paines Plough), **Ghost City** (Sgript Cymru); **Cancer Time** (503); **Sk8** (Theatre Royal, Plymouth); **Big Hopes** (National Assembly), **Amgen:Broken** (Sherman Cymru); **In the Pipeline** (Òran Mór/ Paines Plough); **Blackthorn** (Clywd Theatr Cymru); **Mary Twice** (Bridgend Youth); **Bulletproof** (Replay, Belfast).

Adaptations include: **La Ronde** (Royal Welsh School of Music & Drama); **A Christmas Carol** (Sherman Cymru).

TV includes: **Baker Boys** (co-writer/ creator).

Awards include: **Meyer Whitworth Award, George Devine Award** (The Shadow of a Boy); **Fringe First, Pearson Best Play Award** (The Drowned World).

Gary is a Creative Associate at Watford Palace Theatre.

Morfydd Clark (Jen)

Theatre includes: **Blodeuwedd** (Theatr Genedlaethol Cymru).

Television includes: **Arthur & George, A Poet in New York, New Worlds.**

Film includes: **Love & Friendship, The Call Up, Pride & Prejudice & Zombies, The Falling, Madame Bovary, Two Missing.**

Cai Dyfan (Designer)

For the Royal Court, film includes: **Off the Page** (& Guardian).

As Designer, theatre includes: **The Passion, The Village Social** (National Theatre Wales); **Paul Bunyan** (WNO); **Sgint, Trwy'r Ddinas Hon** (Sherman Cymru); **Rhwng Dau Fyd, Chwalfa** (Theatr Genedlaethol Cymru); **After the End** (Dirty Protest); **Your Last Breath** (Curious Detective); **Wasted** (Paines Plough/Birmingham Rep/ Latitude/tour).

As Associate Designer, theatre includes: **The Lion, the Witch & the Wardrobe** (Kensington Gardens); **How the Whale Became** (ROH); **A Life of Galileo** (RSC); **A Number** (Nuffield, Southampton); **Mr Burns** (Almeida); **King Charles III** (Almeida/West End); **Medea** (National).

As Art Director, television includes: **Convenience.** As Assistant Art Director, television includes: **Hinterland/Y Gwyll.**

Jessica Harwood (Production Manager)

Theatre includes: **The Royale, Albion, Perseverance Drive, We are Proud to Present, The Herd, Josephine & I, Disgraced, Money the Gameshow** (Bush).

Previously, Jess worked as Project Manager for the build of the new Bush Theatre

Jason Hughes (Rick)

For the Royal Court: **4.48 Psychosis** (US tour), **A Real Classy Affair.**

Other theatre includes: **Way Upstream** (Chichester Festival); **In the Next Room/ The Vibrator Play** (St James); **Design for Living, The Fight for Barbara** (Theatre Royal, Bath); **Caligula, Badfinger** (Donmar); **Kiss Me Like You Mean It** (Soho); **In Flame** (West End); **Look Back in Anger** (National); **The Herbal Bed** (The Other Place); **Snake in the Grass** (Old Vic); **The Illusion** (Royal Exchange, Manchester); **Nothing to Pay** (BAC); **Macbeth** (Theatr Clwyd); **The Unexpected Guest** (Windsor).

Television includes: **Archer, Midsomer Murders, Pornography, This Life 10 Years On, Mine All Mine, Waking the Dead, Plain Jane, The Harry Enfield Show, The Flint Street Nativity, Thin Air, This Life, King Girl, Stranger in the Night.**

Film includes: **Crow, Mabel, Dead Long Enough, Dante's Daemon, Dirty Bomb, Say Sorry, Calling the Shots, Jimmy Fizz, Killing Me Softly, Fear of Falling, Shooters, House, Ill Communication.**

Mark Melville (Composer & Sound Designer)

For the Royal Court: **God Bless the Child**

Other theatre includes: **Yer Granny, Knives in Hens, Miracle Man, Empty, My Shrinking Life** (National Theatre of Scotland); **Tomorrow** (Vanishing Point/Cena

Contemporânea Festival, Brasil/Brighton Festival/Tramway/National); Dragon (Vox Motus/National Theatre of Scotland/Tianjin People's Art Theatre, China); The Beautiful Cosmos of Ivor Cutler (Vanishing Point/National Theatre of Scotland); Swallows & Amazons, Grimm Tales (Theatre by the Lake); Saturday Night (Vanishing Point/National Theatre of Portugal); Pride & Prejudice (Two Bit Classics); Mister Holgado (Unicorn); A Midsummer Night's Dream (Royal Lyceum, Edinburgh); Wonderland (Vanishing Point/Napoli Teatro Festival Italia/Tramway/Edinburgh International Festival); Mwana (Ankur/Tron);

The Beggars Opera (Vanishing Point/Royal Lyceum, Edinburgh/Belgrade, Coventry); What Happened Was This, One Night Stand, Naked Neighbour Twitching Blind (Never Did Nothing/Tron/Tramway); Hamlet, Your Country Needs You (but I don't need my country), No Fat Juliets, Robin Hood, Pierrepoint, The Unsociables, The BFG, Two, Merlin, Quicksand, The Snow Queen, Peter Pan, Children of Killers, Of Mice & Men, Jason & The Argonauts (Dukes Playhouse).

Dance Includes: In a Deep Dark Wood (Gobbledegook/Moko Dance); Best Friends (M6/Ludus).

Awards Include: Critics Award for Theatre for Best Technical Presentation (Dragon); Critics Award for Theatre for Best Music & Sound (The Beautiful Cosmos of Ivor Cutler); UK Theatre Award for Best Show for Children & Young People (Mister Holgado).

Mark is an Associate Artist of The Dukes Playhouse.

David Moorst (Liam)

Theatre includes: Wonderland (Hampstead).

Television includes: Partners in Crime, Holby City.

Siwan Morris (Suze)

For the Royal Court: Gas Station Angel.

Other theatre includes: Tonypandemonium, A Good Night Out in the Valleys (National Theatre Wales); Cloakroom (Sherman Cymru); Knives in Hens (Theatre Royal, Bath); A Midsummer Night's Dream, Suddenly Last Summer, The Rabbit, King Lear, Flora's War, Hosts of Rebecca, The Journey Of Mary Kelly, Rape of the Fair Country, Equus (Theatr Clwyd); The Seagull (Bristol Old Vic); Much Ado About Nothing, Twelfth Night (UK tour); The Merchant of Venice, The Winter's Tale (Ludlow Festival).

Television includes: Y Streica Fi, Doctor Who, Our Girl, Wolfblood, Holby City, Whites, Caerdydd, Con Passionate, Miss Marple, Skins, Antigone, Mine All Mine, 20 Things To Do Before You're 30, Belonging, Social Action, The Bill, The Marvellous Handshake, Casualty, Mind To Kill, The Bench, Sister Lulu, Sucker Fish, Tales of the Pleasure Beach.

Film includes: Dark Signal, The Devil's Vice, The Machine.

Radio includes: Summer is Long to Come, Dylan Thomas Shorts, Dover & the Unkindest Cut of All, On Top of the World, Same As it Ever Was, Station Road, The True Memoirs of Harriett Wilson.

Hamish Pirie (Director)

For the Royal Court: Who Cares, Teh Internet is Serious Business.

Other theatre includes: I'm With The Band (Traverse/Wales Millennium Centre); Quiz Show, Demos, 50 Plays for Edinburgh (Traverse); Love With A Capital 'L', 3 Seconds, Most Favoured, The Last Bloom (Traverse/Òran Mór); Bravo Figaro (ROH/Traverse); Salt Root & Roe (Donmar/Trafalgar Studios); Purgatory (Arcola); Stacy (Arcola/Trafalgar); Pennies (nabokov); Paper House (Flight 5065).

Hamish trained as Resident Assistant Director at Paines Plough and at the Donmar Warehouse. He was previously Associate Director at the Traverse Theatre. Hamish is an Associate Director at the Royal Court.

Lizzie Powell (Lighting Designer)

For the Royal Court: Open Court.

Other theatre includes: Fever Dream: Southside, The Libertine, Far Away/Seagulls, Krapp's Last Tape/Footfalls (Citizens); Anna Karenina (Royal Exchange, Manchester/West Yorkshire Playhouse); Secret Theatre (Lyric, Hammersmith/tour); In A Time O' Strife, Glasgow Girls, My Shrinking Life, The Enquirer, An Appointment with the Wickerman, Knives in Hens, Girl X, Transform Glasgow, Transform Orkney, Mary Queen of Scots Got Her Head Chopped Off, Our Teacher's a Troll, Rupture, Venus as a Boy, The Recovery Position (National Theatre of Scotland); White Gold (Iron Oxide); Idomeneus (Gate); Cinderella, Mother Goose, Jack & the Beanstalk (Perth); Caged, Poppy & Dingan, The Book of Beasts (Catherine Wheels); Spring Awakening, While You Lie, Any Given Day, The Dark

Things (Traverse); Mr Snow, The Night
Before Christmas (Macrobert); Pangaa
(Ankur); Huxley's Lab (Grid Iron/Lung
Ha's/Edinburgh Festival Theatre);
Treasure Island (Wee Stories); Under
Milk Wood (Theatre Royal, Northampton);
The Death of Harry Leon, Making History
(Ouroborous, Dublin); Cockroach, The
Dogstone/Nasty, Brutish & Short, Nobody
Will Ever Forgive Us (National Theatre of
Scotland/Traverse); The Wasp Factory
(Cumbernauld); Great Expectations
(Prime); Travels With My Aunt (New
Wolsey).

Roy Alexander Weise (Assistant Director)

As Assistant Director, for the Royal Court: **Who Cares, Liberian Girl.**

As Director, other theatre includes: **PLUNDER (Young Vic); Palindrome (Arcola); EMPIRES (Bush); The Man in the Green Jacket (Jermyn Street); What Happens Behind the Bar (Cockpit); SKEEN! (OvalHouse); Invisible Mice (Lyric Lounge); Seventeen (Rose Bruford College); Chameleon (Unicorn).**

As Assistant Director, other theatre includes: **Albion, We Are Proud to Present... (Bush); Public Enemy, Hamlet, The Government Inspector (Young Vic); The Serpent's Tooth (Almeida/Talawa).**

As Trainee Director, television includes: **INVISIBLE.**

Roy is currently the Trainee Director at the Royal Court.

JUN – JUL 2015

JERWOOD THEATRE
DOWNSTAIRS

11 Jun - 18 Jul
hang
written and directed by
debbie tucker green

A crime has been committed.
The victim has a choice to make.
The criminal is waiting.

A shattering new play about one
woman's unspeakable decision.
debbie tucker green (RANDOM,
TRUTH AND RECONCILIATION) returns to
the Royal Court to direct her
new play.

The cast includes Marianne Jean-
Baptiste who makes her Royal
Court debut alongside Claire
Rushbrook and Shane Zaza.

JERWOOD THEATRE
UPSTAIRS

18 - 25 Jul
Primetime

A series of new short plays
written by primary school
children aged 8 – 11.

Immediately following a free
tour of London primary schools
in the summer term of 2015,
this production of eight short
plays will run at the Royal
Court alongside free family
playwriting workshops.

PRIMETIME is supported by John Lyon's Charity,
The Mercers' Company, The Haberdashers'
Company, Ernest Cook Trust, John Thaw
Foundation, Royal Victoria Hall Foundation and
The Austin and Hope Pilkington Trust.

Age guidance 7+

ON TOUR

Until 4 Jul
Constellations
by Nick Payne

Following critically acclaimed,
sold-out runs in the West
End and on Broadway,
Constellations embarks
on its first tour.

★ ★ ★ ★ ★
"Extraordinary. Dazzling."
Independent

14 – 16 May
New Victoria Theatre, Woking

19 – 23 May
Liverpool Playhouse

27 – 30 May
Bristol Old Vic

2 – 6 Jun
Nuffield Theatre, Southampton

9 – 13 Jun
The Lowry, Salford Quays

16 – 20 Jun
Cambridge Arts Theatre

23 – 27 Jun
Richmond Theatre

30 Jun – 4 Jul
Theatre Royal Brighton

Constellations was first staged in 2012 as part
of the Royal Court's Jerwood New Playwrights
programme, supported by the Jerwood
Charitable Foundation.

020 7565 5000 (no booking fee)
royalcourttheatre.com

Follow us ✷ royalcourt ⨍ royalcourttheatre
Royal Court Theatre Sloane Square London, SW1W 8AS

THE ROYAL COURT THEATRE

The Royal Court Theatre is the writers' theatre. It is the leading force in world theatre for energetically cultivating writers – undiscovered, new, and established.

Through the writers the Royal Court is at the forefront of creating restless, alert, provocative theatre about now, inspiring audiences and influencing future writers. Through the writers the Royal Court strives to constantly reinvent the theatre ecology, creating theatre for everyone.

We invite and enable conversation and debate, allowing writers and their ideas to reach and resonate beyond the stage, and the public to share in the thinking.

Over 120,000 people visit the Royal Court in Sloane Square, London, each year and many thousands more see our work elsewhere through transfers to the West End and New York, national and international tours, residencies across London and site-specific work.

The Royal Court's extensive development activity encompasses a diverse range of writers and artists and includes an ongoing programme of writers' attachments, readings, workshops and playwriting groups. Twenty years of pioneering work around the world means the Royal Court has relationships with writers on every continent.

The Royal Court opens its doors to radical thinking and provocative discussion, and to the unheard voices and free thinkers that, through their writing, change our way of seeing.

Within the past sixty years, John Osborne, Arnold Wesker and Howard Brenton have all started their careers at the Court. Many others, including Caryl Churchill, Mark Ravenhill and Sarah Kane have followed. More recently, the theatre has found and fostered new writers such as Polly Stenham, Mike Bartlett, Bola Agbaje, Nick Payne and Rachel De-lahay and produced many iconic plays from Laura Wade's **Posh** to Bruce Norris' **Clybourne Park** and Jez Butterworth's **Jerusalem**. Royal Court plays from every decade are now performed on stage and taught in classrooms across the globe.

It is because of this commitment to the writer that we believe there is no more important theatre in the world than the Royal Court.

Supported using public funding by
**ARTS COUNCIL
ENGLAND**

ROYAL COURT SUPPORTERS

The Royal Court is a registered charity and not-for-profit company. We need to raise £1.7 million every year in addition to our core grant from the Arts Council and our ticket income to achieve what we do.

We have significant and longstanding relationships with many generous organisations and individuals who provide vital support. Royal Court supporters enable us to remain the writers' theatre, find stories from everywhere and create theatre for everyone.

We can't do it without you.

Coutts supports Innovation at the Royal Court. The Genesis Foundation supports the Royal Court's work with International Playwrights. Alix Partners support The Big Idea at the Royal Court. Bloomberg supports Beyond the Court. The Jerwood Charitable Foundation supports emerging writers through the Jerwood New Playwrights series. The Pinter Commission is given annually by his widow, Lady Antonia Fraser, to support a new commission at the Royal Court.

PUBLIC FUNDING

Arts Council England, London
British Council

CHARITABLE DONATIONS

The Austin & Hope
  Pilkington Trust
Martin Bowley Charitable Trust
Ernest Cook Trust
Cowley Charitable Trust
The Dorset Foundation
The Eranda Foundation
Lady Antonia Fraser for
  The Pinter Commission

Genesis Foundation
The Golden Bottle Trust
The Haberdashers' Company
Roderick & Elizabeth Jack
Jerwood Charitable
Foundation
Marina Kleinwort Trust
The Andrew Lloyd Webber
Foundation
John Lyon's Charity
Clare McIntyre's Bursary
The Andrew W. Mellon
Foundation
The Mercers' Company
The David & Elaine Potter
Foundation
Rose Foundation
Royal Victoria Hall Foundation
The Sackler Trust
The Sobell Foundation
John Thaw Foundation
The Vandervell Foundation
Sir Siegmund Warburg's
Voluntary Settlement
The Garfield Weston
Foundation
The Wolfson Foundation

CORPORATE SPONSORS

AKA
AlixPartners
Aqua Financial Solutions Ltd
Bloomberg
Colbert
Coutts
Fever-Tree
Gedye & Sons
MAC
Nyetimber

BUSINESS MEMBERS

Annoushka
Auerbach & Steele
  Opticians
CNC – Communications &
  Network Consulting
Cream
Heal's
Lazard
Salamanca Group
Tetragon Financial Group
Vanity Fair

DEVELOPMENT ADVOCATES

Piers Butler
Sindy Caplan
Sarah Chappatte
Cas Donald (Vice Chair)
Celeste Fenichel
Piers Gibson
Emma Marsh (Chair)
Deborah Shaw
  (Vice Chair)
Tom Siebens
Sian Westerman

INDIVIDUAL SUPPORTERS

Major Donors
Eric Abraham
Ray Barrell & Ursula Van Almsick
Cas Donald
Lydia & Manfred Gorvy
Richard & Marcia Grand
Jack & Linda Keenan
Adam Kenwright
Mandeep Manku
Miles Morland
Mr & Mrs Sandy Orr
NoraLee & Jon Sedmak
Deborah Shaw & Stephen Marquardt
Jan & Michael Topham
Monica B Voldstad

Mover-Shakers
Anonymous
Jordan Cook
Piers & Melanie Gibson
Duncan Matthews QC
Ian & Carol Sellars

Boundary-Breakers
Anonymous
Katie Bradford
David Harding
Roderick & Elizabeth Jack
Nicola Kerr
Philip & Joan Kingsley
Emma Marsh
Rachel Mason
Angelie & Shafin Moledina
Andrew & Ariana Rodger

Ground-Breakers
Anonymous
Moira Andreae
Mr & Mrs Simon Andrews
Nick Archdale
Elizabeth & Adam Bandeen
Michael Bennett
Sam & Rosie Berwick
Dr Kate Best
Christopher Bevan
Sarah & David Blomfield
Deborah Brett
Peter & Romey Brown
Clive & Helena Butler
Piers Butler
Sindy & Jonathan Caplan

Gavin & Lesley Casey
Sarah & Philippe Chappatte
Tim & Caroline Clark
Clyde Cooper
Ian & Caroline Cormack
Mr & Mrs Cross
Andrew & Amanda Cryer
Alison Davies
Roger & Alison De Haan
Matthew Dean
Sarah Denning
Polly Devlin OBE
Rob & Cherry Dickins
Denise & Randolph Dumas
Robyn Durie
Glenn & Phyllida Earle
Graham & Susanna Edwards
Mark & Sarah Evans
Sally & Giles Everist
Celeste & Peter Fenichel
Margy Fenwick
The Edwin Fox Foundation
Dominic & Claire Freemantle
Beverley Gee
Nick & Julie Gould
Lord & Lady Grabiner
Jill Hackel & Andrzej Zarzycki
Carol Hall
Maureen Harrison
Sam & Caroline Haubold
David & Sheila Hodgkinson
Mr & Mrs Gordon Holmes
Kate Hudspeth
Damien Hyland
Suzie & David Hyman
Amanda & Chris Jennings
Melanie J Johnson
Nicholas Jones
Susanne Kapoor
David P Kaskel
  & Christopher A Teano
Vincent & Amanda Keaveny
Peter & Maria Kellner
Mr & Mrs Pawel Kisielewski
David & Sarah Kowitz
Daisy & Richard Littler
Kathryn Ludlow
Dr Ekaterina Malievskaia
  & George Goldsmith
Christopher Marek Rencki
Mr & Mrs Marsden
Mrs Janet Martin
Andrew McIver
David & Elizabeth Miles
Barbara Minto
Takehito Mitsui

M. Murphy Altschuler
Peter & Maggie Murray-Smith
Ann & Gavin Neath CBE
Clive & Annie Norton
Kate O'Neill
Jonathan Och & Rita Halbright
Georgia Oetker
Adam Oliver-Watkins
Anatol Orient
Sir William & Lady Vanessa Patey
Andrea & Hilary Ponti
Annie & Preben Prebensen
Greg & Karen Reid
Paul & Gill Robinson
Sir Paul & Lady Ruddock
William & Hilary Russell
Sally & Anthony Salz
Tom Siebens & Mimi Parsons
Dr Wendy Sigle
Andy Simpkin
Brian Smith
Saadi & Zeina Soudavar
The Ulrich Family
Constanze Von Unruh
Matthew & Sian Westerman
Mrs Alexandra Whiley
Anne-Marie Williams
Sir Robert & Lady Wilson
Katherine & Michael Yates

With thanks to our Friends, Stage-Taker, Ice-Breaker and Future Court members whose support we greatly appreciate.

Innovation partner

Supported using public funding by

ARTS COUNCIL ENGLAND

EMPLOYEES
THE ROYAL COURT & ENGLISH STAGE COMPANY

Remember the Royal Court in your will and help to ensure that our future is as iconic as our past.

Every gift, whatever the amount, will help us maintain and care for the building, support the next generation of playwrights starting out in their career, deliver our education programme and put our plays on the stage.

To discuss leaving a legacy to the Royal Court, please contact:

Sue Livermore, Senior Individual Giving Manager, Royal Court Theatre, Sloane Square, London, SW1W 8AS

Email: suelivermore@royalcourttheatre.com
Tel: 020 7565 5079

VIOLENCE AND SON

Gary Owen

VIOLENCE AND SON

OBERON BOOKS
LONDON

WWW.OBERONBOOKS.COM

First published in 2015 by Oberon Books Ltd
521 Caledonian Road, London N7 9RH
Tel: +44 (0) 20 7607 3637 / Fax: +44 (0) 20 7607 3629
e-mail: info@oberonbooks.com
www.oberonbooks.com

A catalogue record for this book is available from the British
Library.

PB ISBN: 9781783198931
E ISBN: 9781783198948

Printed, bound and converted
by CPI Group (UK) Ltd, Croydon, CR0 4YY.

for Brigid Larmour,
without whom I would have given all this up long ago

Thanks to Vicky and the Classic Paines Plough line-up for sticking with me. To Chris Campbell for a lovely pub lunch. And to Helen Raynor Ltd., for keeping me in a manner to which I am gradually becoming accustomed.

Characters

LIAM, seventeen.

JEN, eighteen.

SUZE, thirties.

RICK, forties.

All but LIAM have south Wales accents.

A forward slash in a speech ('/') indicates the
point at which the next speech should begin.

SCENE ONE

A living room in a flat above a convenience store. Beyond, a small Valleys town. Beyond that, all of Time and Space.

LIAM enters. He is dressed as Matt Smith's Doctor. Fez, bow tie, the lot.

He stops. Looks round the place, wary.

He gets out a sonic screwdriver. Tries to scan the room. But there's something wrong with the sonic.

JEN: *(From off.)* And?

LIAM: Sonic's being temperamental. Hold on.

> *He fiddles with the sonic screwdriver.*

LIAM: If I can just reverse the polarity of the – yes!

> *And now the sonic lights up, whines and buzzes. LIAM scans the room.*
>
> *Inspects the reading on the sonic screwdriver.*
>
> *Draws a conclusion.*
>
> *And then he stops performing. Turns back to the door he came in through.*

LIAM: Yeah we're alright. Pissed bastard'll be down the York by now.

> *JEN enters, dressed as Amy Pond, dressed as a WPC strippogram, as in 'The Eleventh Hour'. Wig of long red hair, white shirt, chequered tie, stab proof vest, and a very short skirt. She looks round at the room. Liam watches her for a bit, then –*

LIAM: So it's not exactly Buckingham Palace.

JEN: Well I wouldn't know.

LIAM: I'll take you one day. Queen does a lovely tea, actually. Nice scones. Not stingy with the cream.

JEN: I wouldn't be seen dead with that entitled bitch.

LIAM: Nah, fair enough…

> *He goes to pick up a DVD box.*

LIAM: …she is a bit of a cunt.

He's getting a disc out, giving it a bit of a wipe clean.

He stops.

LIAM: I feel bad now, calling the Queen a cunt.

JEN: Showing off a bit.

LIAM: D'you think?

JEN: Slightly.

LIAM: As an old lady – fine. I got no problem with her. I'm not calling *her* a – she's someone's mum.

JEN: I get it.

LIAM: I'm not the kind of person, would call an old lady a cunt.

JEN: It's the institution –

LIAM: Yes!

JEN: – which is completely cunty.

LIAM: With you, sister.

He offers her a fist to bump.

She looks at it.

Looks at him. He's very serious. Though obviously messing.

She bumps his first.

He turns away. She's smiling about him a bit as he talks.

LIAM: So we'll start with *Rose*, where we meet the Ninth Doctor. And of course Rose. And obviously… first ep of a reboot, lot to get done, lots of characters and concepts to introduce, and to be fair, Davies doesn't do a bad job of it.

JEN: In your humble opinion…

LIAM: I just can't believe you call youself a fan, and you've never seen Christopher Eccleston's Doctor.

JEN: I don't call myself a fan.

LIAM: She says, got up like Amy Pond.

JEN: I like the outfit.

LIAM: *I* like the outfit. And the skirt's…

JEN: What's up with my skirt, Liam?

LIAM: *(Can almost not say it.)* …apart from the hem?

JEN: Is it causing you problems?

LIAM crumbles, turns away.

LIAM: …besides, you know Russell T Davies is actually on record as saying, he's aiming at the 8-year-old kids in the audience?

JEN: It is a kids' show…

LIAM: Family show. Different thing.

JEN: Families include kids.

LIAM: I'm just saying, with RTD, he's writing for the 8 year olds… and you can tell. Whereas with Moffat…

JEN: Yeah but I liked David Tennant.

LIAM: Hey hey hey I am not slagging off David Tennant, David Tennant's easily the third best Doctor ever, don't get me wrong.

JEN: Just with the Matt Smith stuff…it's really good but half the time I'm trying to remember, where in River Song's timeline are we –

LIAM: So it's shit cos you don't understand it?

JEN: Did I say it was shit?

LIAM: About five seconds ago.

JEN: I said it's really good but.

LIAM: Which equals shit.

JEN: It equals really good. But.

LIAM: Why don't we, after we've done the Ninth Doctor, we could always watch the Matt Smith years again, together, and I'll explain it as we're going along, and I really think once you see how Moffat's vision all comes together –

JEN: Yeah alright.

LIAM: Yeah?

JEN: Yeah, give it another chance. I might get it this time.

LIAM: Okay. So… good.

JEN: With you to explain it to me.

He looks at her: she's deadpan.

LIAM: So let's start with Rose.

JEN: I like Rose.

LIAM: Okay good –

JEN: Cos she's a girl, like me, she's into mascara and boys so there's stuff I can like relate to, unlike the other stuff about time paradoxes, cos how do I relate to time paradoxes when I spend all my empty life hanging round the make-up counter at Superdrug?

LIAM: I was just saying –

JEN: D'you have dreams where you bump into Steven Moffat on a train and you and him become mates cos you're the only one who really gets what he's trying to do? And he emails you ideas at three in the morning when / he's just not sure…

LIAM: Yeah, alright.

JEN: Is it? Is it alright for me to like some things but then not like others so much?

LIAM: *(Beat.)* As long as you keep your massively faulty opinions to yourself, yes that's acceptable.

LIAM reaches for the remote.

Stabs at it, with a bit of flourish and ceremony.

The remote doesn't work.

LIAM: Jesus…

He takes off the battery cover, rolls the batteries around.

Tries again.

LIAM: I told him to get new batteries last week.

JEN: Just shift your arse press the buttons on the machine.

He's still trying. No good.

LIAM: Give it a sec.

He picks up the sonic. Sonics the remote.

LIAM: *(Off JEN's look.)* On my life, one time it worked.

He tries the remote again. Nothing.

JEN: But not this time...

He gets up. Goes to the DVD player.

LIAM: It'll take a while thinking about it.

JEN: Liam.

LIAM: Yeah?

JEN: I didn't, really...

She dries up.

LIAM: What?

JEN: Come *on,* mun.

LIAM: *What?*

JEN: D'you think I really came here with you to watch *Dr Who?*

Brings LIAM to a halt.

LIAM: Right. Okay.

He closes his eyes, breathes deep, in a very controlled way.

JEN: You alright?

LIAM: *(Eyes still shut.)* Fine.

JEN: I do want to watch *Dr Who,* even the really old stuff from the Nineties –

LIAM's eyes snap open.

LIAM: You should, McCoy is *massively* underrated.

JEN: But I came here today for another reason.

LIAM: I was sort of... hoping it might be, for another reason.

JEN: D'you know what that reason was?

LIAM: I could sort of guess? But then if I got it wrong, it'd be horribly embarrassing so I think I'd just as well / you told me.

JEN: The reason was you.

LIAM: Well that's sort, yeah, what I – okay. Good.

JEN: Cos – there's you. By here.

She points to a spot in front of her.

JEN: There's all the other boys. B'there.

She points to a spot far from the first.

So I'm saying you're very very different.

LIAM: Do you think I'm secretly a vampire?

JEN: I haven't ruled it out.

LIAM: I'm different... in some ways. Not all ways.

JEN: In good ways.

LIAM: I'll take that.

JEN: Compared to lads round here, it *is* like you landed in a blue box from another planet.

LIAM: It feels like I did, a lot of the time.

JEN: I mean I can really talk to you. The boys round here – they basically just grunt.

LIAM: Yeah isn't that Welsh?

JEN: Quite a cheap joke...

LIAM: Cheap jokes are best, you get so much more for your money.

JEN: And almost racist.

LIAM: That'll be why it's so cheap, no one's doing racism these days, it's really – no one's into it now.

JEN: I am genuinely trying to be serious, so you might wanna – just see if you can respond to me on that sort of level, at all?

LIAM: Yes, alright, okay? I felt it too. First time we talked. It was like we were really –

JEN: Talking.

LIAM: As shit as that sounds.

JEN: I'm actually a bit nervous now.

LIAM: *You* are?

JEN: It's quite a big deal, what I want to ask you.

LIAM: It's a yes.

JEN: You don't know what I'm gonna ask.

LIAM: I don't need to. Oh Jesus. Jesus *Christ…*

He shakes himself out.

LIAM: Whatever you ask, it's a yes. Yes. Definitely yes.

JEN: Well that's – that's… you *sweetheart.*

They look at each other.

JEN: So.

LIAM: So…

JEN: D'you think Jordan really likes me or does he not?

LIAM: Sorry?

JEN: Does Jordan like me, or is he not that bothered?

LIAM: Oh okay.

JEN: Because like – typical Saturday night, right? We go to the pub: he talks to his mates, I talk to my mates. We go to a party: he talks to his mates, I talk to my mates. We get pissed: he wanders over, sticks his tongue down my throat and his hand down my jeans. And that's great as far as it goes. But it's not what I dreamed of, as a little girl.

LIAM: No I can imagine.

JEN: And my friends say – basically they're saying, he's out of my league and I'm… Tina actually at one point said it might be mistaken identity, that he thinks I'm someone else? Someone… better.

LIAM: How could that be?

JEN: Well cos everyone thinks Jordan's brilliant, like, really great body and not a twat and he's getting this development contract with the Ospreys next year?

LIAM: I have no idea what that means.

JEN: It means they'll pay him, to play rugby. That'll be his job.

LIAM: You can get paid to play rugby?

JEN: I don't think anyone would play it for fun.

LIAM: No, fair point.

She thinks. She gets hopeful... and then sad. LIAM watches, rap.

JEN: Like one time I said, Jord, I've watched you play loads, let's do something I like. He said yeah great no problem. So he came round, and we were gonna watch *The Girl Who Waited* –

LIAM: Did he keep asking you who everyone was?

JEN: No we were cwtched, for like five minutes – and then he peels me off starts doing one-handed press-ups. And I'm like, sorry what? And he goes oh I'm still watching your programme. And he was. But like the whole of the episode, he's doing upper body work. And it's –

LIAM: It's not is it...

JEN: – is that romance, seriously?

She stops.

JEN: So he doesn't express an interest in me, as a person, cos... he hasn't got one.

LIAM shrugs.

JEN: I should just finish it then probably.

LIAM: If you've not got anything in common, then...

JEN: So that's what you think? I should finish with Jordan?

LIAM: Well I can't really say can I.

JEN: Why, what broke your mouth?

LIAM: It's not fair, for me to say.

JEN: Oh God, what'm I gonna do? Just even the idea of doing it is making me all tense. I can feel it now my back and shoulders tensing up.

LIAM: Well just… calm down then.

JEN: How can I calm down?

LIAM: Stop thinking about it?

JEN: I'm gonna get a migraine, I swear to God. That's two days in a dark room puking my guts out, and I haven't even done it yet.

LIAM: Is there anything I can do?

JEN: Like what?

LIAM: I was sort of asking you?

JEN: Got any pharmaceutical grade morphine?

LIAM: Just out, sorry.

JEN: I can feel it. I'm gonna puke. Any kind of emotional overload, you know, I'm chucking everywhere.

LIAM: I could give you a rub?

JEN: Beg your pardon?

LIAM: Like, your shoulders. I could rub your shoulders for you. Might help.

JEN: I think we're a bit beyond that.

LIAM: It's just you said it's your shoulders tensing up starts it off.

JEN: Yeah, but unless you've got magic fingers –

LIAM: Just… my mum. When she'd get stressed out. I'd rub her shoulders, and she said it helped. Even right at the end.

It takes JEN a moment to respond.

JEN: That'd be really nice yeah.

LIAM: Okay. Do you wanna –

JEN: What shall I sit on the floor?

LIAM: Yeah okay. Or if I sit first?

LIAM sits down on the settee. JEN sits on the floor, in front of him. She leans her head forward.

LIAM: Okay. Right.

JEN: What?

LIAM: You might have to um – take off the stab-proof vest.

JEN: Sure you're not gonna stab me?

LIAM: I think you're safe.

She considers. Looks at him.

JEN: I reckon I am.

Takes off the stab-proof vest. Sits again.

LIAM begins to knead her shoulders. Gently at first, nervous of touching her. But then more confident.

LIAM: Say if it's too hard.

JEN: It's nice.

He puts a bit more into it.

JEN leans her head forward.

LIAM: That alright?

JEN: Mmm.

He begins to elaborate his technique – kneading with his thumbs just each side of her backbone.

JEN: That is amazing…

LIAM carries on.

Suddenly JEN looks up.

JEN: It's not making you think of your mum is it?

LIAM: How?

JEN: You said you used to do this for your mum. It's not upsetting you is it? Making you think of her.

LIAM: *(Beat.)* This is not making me think about my mum, I promise you that.

JEN: I just didn't wanna, you know. Upset you.

LIAM: You're not.

LIAM goes on working.

And then there's something a little bit fierce, or intense, about his kneading.

JEN looks up. LIAM calms it down, but carries on working.

JEN: Lee.

LIAM: Yeah.

JEN: When I asked, should I finish with Jordan, you said, you couldn't say, because it wouldn't be fair. What did you mean?

LIAM: Just, you're a free individual, you make your own decisions, who the hell do I think I am telling you how to live your life?

JEN: I asked for your advice.

LIAM: Advice, oppression…where d'you draw the line?

She moves away from him.

JEN: You said, it wouldn't be fair. How's it not fair, for you to tell me what you think?

LIAM: Oh come off it.

JEN: Come off what?

LIAM: You know.

JEN: I bloody don't.

LIAM: It wouldn't be fair for me to say, cos…

He steels himself. Big confession.

LIAM: Cos obviously I want you to finish with him.

JEN makes a show of putting it together. There are about three stages. Then –

JEN: D'you fancy me?

LIAM: …do we have to give it a label?

JEN: You bloody do, you fancy me!

19

LIAM: You know what the Buddhists say, about feelings?

JEN: Why the fuck would I / know that –

LIAM: *(Cutting in.)* Feelings are like weather. They float in. They float away. That's all they are. Nothing to get worked up about.

JEN stares at him.

JEN: Do you think about what it'd be like to shag me?

LIAM can't answer immediately. Then –

LIAM: No…

JEN: You're thinking about it now!

LIAM: Cos you put it in my head!

JEN: I thought we were mates.

LIAM: We are, really good mates.

JEN: I came back here, to your place, the two of us – cos I thought we were mates and *nothing more*. I've got a boyfriend!

LIAM: …who you've been telling me you want to dump?

JEN: And you were hardly going all out telling me not to.

LIAM: Well I'm not an idiot…

JEN: Hold on – so, when you were –

She breaks off.

JEN: When you were touching me, just now. Was there… a sexual element?

LIAM: Absolutely none at all.

JEN: I definitely felt a sexual element.

LIAM: In what sort of a way?

JEN: A sexual element – in your touch.

LIAM: Obviously, it was not a horrible thing for me, touching you. But I would never, never – d'you think that's the kind of person I am?

JEN: Well I –

From off-stage – a bang. Wood against a wall.

JEN: What was that?

LIAM: I um –

Another bang. And another. And another. Rhythmic now. Carrying on as they speak.

LIAM: I think that maybe –

Bang. Bang. Bang. Getting faster.

LIAM: Maybe Rick is home after all.

JEN: Right.

Bang. Bang. Bang.

LIAM: I might just go let him know we're here…

LIAM heads to the door. The banging louder and faster. As he reaches the door –

SUZE: *(From off.)* Oh that's it, that's it, that's what I want.…

LIAM stops just short of the door.

LIAM: That's Suze, his…

SUZE: *(From off.)* Oh you beautiful big bastard go *on*…

JEN: His?

LIAM: His really good mate.

SUZE: *(From off.)* Oh you are getting there. You are getting there. You are getting there.

LIAM: Right so they won't be long now.

SUZE: *(From off.)* You are getting there oh *FUCK*…

The banging peaks: subsides: stops.

JEN: Sounds like he got there.

LIAM: He usually does in the end.

The door opens. SUZE in a dark – coloured dressing gown – thrown around her, not done up. She's talking back into the room she's come from.

SUZE: – cos if it was you it was dripping out of, I don't think you'd be so fucking breezy about it –

LIAM: Right Suze?

SUZE: Fuck!

SUZE pulls the dressing gown tight. It has no belt so she has to hold it shut.

SUZE: Didn't realise you were back.

LIAM: Just walked in the door.

SUZE: Is it?

LIAM: Like one second ago. No more than that at all.

SUZE: *(To JEN.)* Alright, I'm Suze.

JEN: Jen.

SUZE: Like the wig.

JEN: Itches like buggery.

SUZE: Bet it does. I'm just gonna...

She darts over to where a roll of toilet paper sits on a table. Grabs the roll, heads back to the doorway.

SUZE: Won't be a sec now.

Into the bedroom, closes door behind her.

LIAM: So yeah...

LIAM and JEN look at each other.

LIAM: I think, with Suze and Rick, there is quite a strong sexual aspect, to their relationship.

JEN: Well that's nice. I've heard it promotes trust, and intimacy?

LIAM: Aw yeah it's all good stuff.

RICK appears in the door. Bare chest, doing up his belt. He looks at LIAM; at JEN.

RICK: Back alright then.

LIAM: Why wouldn't I be alright?

RICK: Must've been you woke us.

LIAM: Normal people are up by now.

RICK turns to JEN.

RICK: You must be Jen. Since my son hasn't done the introductions.

LIAM: Christ, I'm *so* sorry. Jen, this is my biological male parent, apparently. Though I don't see the resemblance, do you?

RICK: I'm Rick.

JEN: Alright?

LIAM: So that's 'Rick', starting with 'r', not another letter quite close to it in the alphabet.

RICK: Lovely to meet you. At last.

JEN: Yeah and you.

RICK: Good day was it?

JEN: Yeah okay.

RICK: Like the wig.

JEN: Everyone does.

SUZE emerges from the bedroom.

SUZE: Put yourself away love, you'll frighten the girl.

RICK: I'm not frightening anyone, am I?

SUZE finds RICK's top in the room, throws it at him, then finds her handbag, checks herself in a little mirror.

SUZE: Depress the shit out of her then, when she sees what she's got to look forward to in twenty years time.

LIAM smirks at this. RICK notices.

RICK: *(To LIAM.)* Whassat?

LIAM knows there's some piss-taking coming.

LIAM: What is what?

RICK: Round your neck.

LIAM: It's a bow tie.

RICK shakes his head, as if baffled.

LIAM: Are you telling me you've never seen a bow tie before?

RICK: Not in real life no.

LIAM: Bow ties are cool.

RICK: *(Beat.)* No they fucking are not.

LIAM: Well thanks for clearing that up.

SUZE finishes touching up her make-up.

SUZE: So where you been today then?

LIAM: Regenerations.

SUZE – blank.

JEN: It's a conference.

RICK looks to JEN when she speaks; his gaze lingers on her a little.

SUZE: Whassat, save the world sort of thing?

LIAM: Not exactly no.

JEN: It's about *Dr Who.*

SUZE: They have conferences, about *Dr Who?*

LIAM: And science fiction and fantasy more generally.

SUZE: What the fuck for?

LIAM: For fun?

Not immediately after RICK looks away from her, but not long after – and almost without being aware she's doing it – JEN tugs her skirt down a little.

SUZE: A conference: about *Dr Who?* It's wild, the stuff they got these days. *(To LIAM and JEN.)* And what people dress up do they?

LIAM: You don't have to, but it makes it –

SUZE: More fun?

LIAM: Yeah.

SUZE: Do they go as Daleks?

LIAM: That's like the number one thing. Even more than the Doctor.

SUZE: So then what d'they do when they get to stairs?

LIAM: Sorry?

SUZE: If they're a Dalek? And they get to stairs.

JEN: Well: it is just a costume. They've still got their actual legs.

RICK looks over at JEN when she speaks. His gaze lingers on her again.

SUZE: Yeah, course, Suze you twat...

LIAM: Plus Daleks can fly now.

SUZE: You are shitting me? How d'you stop 'em, if they can get up stairs?

LIAM: Madcap genius, or a very big gun.

JEN: 'S alright if I get changed?

LIAM: Yeah, sure.

She picks up her bag.

JEN: So...

...where does she do that?

LIAM: Aw yeah, my room's down there.

JEN: Won't be a sec.

JEN heads off.

SUZE: You're brave.

LIAM: What?

SUZE: You know what state your room's in?

LIAM doesn't, panics: but then remembers. It's fine.

LIAM: It's fine.

SUZE: Apart from all them scrunched up balls of bog roll, piled under the bed?

LIAM stares at her.

SUZE: Don't worry, I cleared them. I shouldn't bloody have to...

LIAM: I've got a cold.

SUZE: It's summer.

LIAM: It's a summer cold.

SUZE: Funny sort of cold makes your snot smell like jizz.

LIAM: Oh my God…

SUZE: Yeah. I said it. Now I don't mind clearing out the plates and the coffee cups with mould in them, but all these wads of tissue paper, all smelling, every so slightly, of bleach – I don't see why I gotta be dealing with that.

LIAM: Don't go in there then.

SUZE: Oh, right. Put 'em back shall I? Still in the black bag in the kitchen, I can if you want, just tip 'em all out in front of that girl of / yours

LIAM: Obviously no

RICK: So what d'you say, then?

LIAM: Cheers Suze, you're a lifesaver.

SUZE: That's better.

Satisfied the point is won, she turns to RICK.

SUZE: He's done well with her hasn't he?

RICK: Father's son.

LIAM: As fucking if.

RICK: How old's she then?

LIAM shrugs.

RICK: Don't gimme the fuckin shrug how old's she?

LIAM: Does it matter?

RICK: Obviously yes or why'd I ask.

LIAM: Eighteen I think.

RICK: Eighteen he thinks? Eighteen he knows.

RICK's smiling.

LIAM: What?

RICK: Older woman. She'll teach you a thing or two...

SUZE: You're embarrassing him...

But she's enjoying teasing him too.

RICK: He embarrasses me enough, going round the place in his paedo outfits. *(To LIAM.)* How'd it go today then? You seal the deal?

LIAM: And what would constitute sealing the deal, in your considered opinion?

RICK: Cop a squeeze?

LIAM: *(Beat.)* Fingered her on the bus.

RICK: You fuckin never? Put it there boy!

LIAM: Course I didn't, you – Jesus...

RICK: She bloody wants it. You know that dunnew.

LIAM: We're just friends.

SUZE: Serious? Nothing going on?

LIAM: We enjoy each other's company. As friends.

RICK: Like fuck.

LIAM: Yeah, I know that's hard for you to process, but, in the twenty-first century, we can manage it quite easily?

RICK: She wear a skirt like that for all her friends?

LIAM: She's not wearing it *for* me. It's a costume.

RICK looks at SUZE, laughs.

RICK: And that's the only costume she could've wore?

LIAM: No, but the Weeping Angel outfit's a bit of faff getting on the bus.

RICK: *(To SUZE.)* Fuck's a Weeping Angel?

SUZE: How the fuck'd I know?

RICK: *(Back to LIAM.)* I'm saying, does she wear stuff like that normally?

LIAM: What, a policewoman's outfit? Hardly ever.

RICK: Skirts like they're fucking belts.

LIAM: Well no –

RICK: There we are then. She fuckin wants it.

LIAM: – she's not normally going to a Dr Who conference, so –

RICK: *(To SUZE.)* Christ Almighty I give up…You have a go?

LIAM: *(Also to SUZE.)* Could you explain to him, not every relationship between a man and a woman is based around shagging.

RICK: You don't fancy her then?

LIAM: Sorry, I was talking to Suze, wasn't I?

SUZE: Lee, you know the summer?

LIAM: No. You're gonna have to remind me.

SUZE: The summer when it's hot.

LIAM: Ah right in theory yes.

SUZE: So it's hot, and you wear shorts. Or whatever you wear. And it's just, you're wearing it cos it suits?

LIAM: Not really a shorts kind of guy myself, I think there's something very sad about grown men dressing like toddlers.

SUZE stares at him, a little weary.

LIAM: But I take your point.

SUZE: When you're a girl, ever since you're ten years old, you put a pair of shorts on, you got blokes eyeing you up. You get to Jen's age, you show some skin, you know what you're doing. Course you do. So she chooses that skirt, on this day, when she's going off with you? That is no fucking accident no way.

LIAM: There is nothing going on between us. She's got a boyfriend.

SUZE: Why's he not taking her?

RICK: Cos he's not a fucking geek.

LIAM: No. He's not. Which is why she's gonna finish with him.

SUZE: So it *was* a bit of a date. Like a pre-date date.

LIAM: No because, she hasn't finished with him yet. But she wanted to go to this conference with me. So long's it's just friends.

SUZE: So she said to you, it had to be, just friends.

LIAM: Yeah.

A look between RICK and SUZE – what is he like?

SUZE: 'S nice of her...

RICK: The things you could learn from me, if you had half the wit...

LIAM: I love that you actually think that's true.

RICK: You know what you've done? You have sold yourself cheap. She wants to go to this thing, doesn't wanna go on her own – so she gets you to come. She gets what she wants. What d'you get? 'Friends'. You should've held out for more. Cos there's more to be had, believe you me.

LIAM: You know a lot about what's going on in the head of this girl you met for two minutes.

RICK turns to SUZE.

RICK: Am I right – or am I right?

SUZE: Sorry – he is, love. It's like – being really honest now – if there's a bloke, and you like him as friend... and you can have him as a friend, and get another bloke as like your bloke as well – you'll have the both. Course you will.

LIAM: No offence now Suze –

SUZE: That's never a good start...

LIAM: – I don't think Jen is like you? In that way? So I don't think what you think really / matters...

RICK: Tell her you won't go with her to any more of this geeky shit, unless it's a date. And if she really wants to go, and there's no – one else to go with her – she'll say yes. You get your date. And then it's everything to play for.

LIAM: I bully her, into going on a date with me? *(To SUZE.)* Was that how it was, with you two?

SUZE: No, it was a bet. And then this place is handy for the pub, so…

RICK: How the fuck's it bullying?

LIAM: Cos I'm telling her she has to do what I say or else.

RICK: No, it's like – you go into a shop. To get some of your fucking… dolls or whatever.

LIAM: Collectable action figures but let it pass.

RICK: And they've got the doll you want, and the price on it's a tenner. So you pay a tenner. Or not, if that's too much for you. 'S no fuckin bullying about it…

SUZE: Just be honest. Tell her what's on your mind.

RICK: He's a teenage boy: what's on his mind is filth.

SUZE: And what d'you think's on a teenage girl's mind, Vile – puppy dogs and ribbons? *(Back to LIAM.)* Don't pretend you're just being mates with her, if really you're not. Cos that's sort of a lie.

LIAM: Okay.

SUZE: Alright.

LIAM: So what exactly does that translate to as action, for me, now?

SUZE: Well I can't tell you what to do, / can I?

RICK: Tell her – that you like her too much to be just friends. You thought you could do it, but you can't. It hurts too much. So if that's all you can ever be to each other… then you can't be with her at all.

SUZE: Where the fuck'd that come from?

RICK gives her a wink.

SUZE: How come you never used the flowery shit on me?

RICK: Was never a need.

He turns to LIAM.

RICK: Just, this once, listen to your old man.

LIAM: I would rather exfoliate my own bollocks, with molten lead. That's not even hyperbole. Hyperbole means wild exaggeration. I'm saying I'd literally do it. I'm saying I'd prefer an agonising death, over listening / to you.

RICK: All I'm saying is, I'm the one getting it on tap twenty-four seven –

SUZE: Oi, you prick...

RICK: – you're the one with the mountain of wank rags under your bed. You think on.

SUZE: D'you have to talk about me like that?

RICK: Like what?

SUZE: Like I'm a hole for you to shoot it into.

RICK: Sweetheart. You are much more than a hole for me to shoot it into...

SUZE already knows where this is going.

RICK: ..you're three, at least.

SUZE: Fuck you – *(Changes tone.)* What d'you mean three at least? What's number four?

RICK: Bloke I knew on the rigs was very fond of an armpit.

SUZE: Armpit's not a hole.

RICK: No, it's... a hollow. You're on those rigs long enough a hollow's all you need.

LIAM picks up JEN approaching.

LIAM: Could you two *please* just –

He breaks off as JEN emerges from LIAM's room, back into civvies.

SUZE: By the way, Jen: it's mould it is. In the walls. Gutter's bust and the damp comes through.

JEN: What now?

SUZE: The smell. It's mould. Not, him.

JEN: Ah, okay. I did wonder.

RICK: So we won't be five minutes then. Suze?

She looks at him – what?

RICK: Off to get chips aren't we?

SUZE: I wish you'd fuckin said...

RICK: I am saying. This is me saying now.

SUZE: I'm sticky as fuck, aren't I.

SUZE is fiddling in her bag.

JEN: You're not getting for me are you?

RICK: Course we are.

JEN: I was just off –

RICK: I'm getting chips anyway. Saturday.

SUZE: But usually you find the way by yourself. With it being two doors down an' all...

SUZE pulls a tiny bottle of perfume from her bag.

SUZE: 'Scuse all.

Sticks it up her top, a burst in the direction of each armpit. Then slightly pulls her leggings away from her stomach, sprays towards her upper thighs. Winces.

RICK: You want anything with your chips Jen?

JEN: Honestly I'm fine.

RICK: Fish? Sausage? Burger? Chicken? Veggie burger? Kebab?

JEN: I'm alright.

RICK: ...rissole?

JEN: I'll just be off I think.

RICK: Don't say I didn't ask.

JEN: I don't think I can.

RICK: Right. See you then.

JEN: Tara.

SUZE: Nice to meet you Jen.

JEN: Yeah and you.

SUZE is gone, RICK lingering. JEN turns away, distracted with some bit of business – check make-up, tie a shoe-lace, pull on a jumper. Anything that means she doesn't see –

RICK, nods at JEN, winks at LIAM.

LIAM shrugs – what the hell's that supposed to mean?

So RICK makes a circle from the index finger and thumb of one hand. Then jabs the index finger of the other hand through it.

LIAM is appalled.

Once RICK is definitely gone.

LIAM: It's actually a lovely story them getting together? They'd been going to the York, for years, getting hammered every Thursday Friday Saturday, but they never actually met? And when they got together they realised three separate times they'd been involved in the same mass brawls, but never met: twice they'd stolen each other's drinks off the bar, but never met; and once had sex in next door cubicles in the bogs – but never actually set eyes on each other?

JEN: Amazing.

LIAM: Isn't it?

JEN: How did they meet in the end then?

LIAM: Internet dating.

They look at each other.

JEN: I had a lovely day.

LIAM: Yeah me too.

She looks around the place.

JEN: I best be off then.

LIAM: If you want.

JEN: Well, just: Jordan'll be wondering.

LIAM: Probably.

JEN: Or maybe not. Maybe won't've noticed. Anyway...

She turns to go.

LIAM: I hope we can do it again. There's a good one in Bristol supposed to be.

JEN: Yeah well.

They look at each other.

JEN: T'ra then.

LIAM: See you.

JEN: See you Liam.

She's going.

LIAM: Is that it?

JEN: Is that what?

LIAM: Is that how our day ends?

JEN: T'ra, see you. Pretty standard.

LIAM shrugs.

JEN: So…

LIAM shrugs again, not looking at her.

JEN: But hasn't it been a lovely day?

LIAM: I said that.

JEN: So don't – you know.

LIAM: Don't what?

JEN: Don't get weird and spoil it.

LIAM: Maybe I am weird. Maybe I've been weird all along and I'm just hiding it. Maybe that's too much for you.

JEN: It's more it's too fuckin boring.

LIAM: Oh well that's me told.

JEN: I don't think you are weird. I don't think dressing up like the Doctor is weird, see. I think it's a laugh. So you're not weird. And don't make yourself be now. Just –

They look at each other.

JEN: Okay. I'll see you very soon.

She goes to leave.

LIAM: No I can't.

JEN: Oh.

LIAM: I can't pretend that's it all fine, and I can't pretend I'm not... feeling certain / things when

JEN: *(Cutting in.)* What then?

LIAM: If we go to another conference, it can't be just as friends. I can't do that.

JEN: So you're telling me, I have to go on a date with you.

LIAM: No, I'm not saying / that

JEN: You are –

LIAM: No!

JEN: You're saying I have to go out with you. On a date. When you know I've got a boyfriend.

LIAM: No!

JEN: How's that gonna work? You gonna tell Jordan for me? Cos I can't see him being too happy about it –

LIAM: I'm not saying you have to do anything, right?

JEN: Fuckin sounds like you are.

LIAM: I'm saying – *all* I'm saying – is about me. It's about what *I'm* gonna do. And I'm not going to be able to go out with you so anything else, and pretend I just wanna be your friend. Alright? Because *(Beat.)* I think I could love you, actually.

JEN just stares at him.

LIAM: Not now, that would be – that would be weird – I'm saying, if we gave it a chance –

JEN: So if I want to carry on being your friend, and nothing more: then I can fuck right off?

LIAM: That's obviously not how I'd put it.

JEN: That *is* how I'm putting it.

LIAM: Well if that's how you *want* to put it, the last thing I want to do is tell you how you can or cannot put things.

JEN: Well then.

She stares at him.

JEN: Okay. So this is me, fucking right off.

She's up and off.

LIAM: What?

And she's gone.

LIAM sits, gob-smacked.

LIAM: Shit.

He gets out his phone. Dials. It gets busied. Answerphone.

Tries again. It gets busied.

LIAM: Yeah Jen will you answer please.

He sits for a bit.

Tries her number again. Rings off as soon as he gets answerphone.

And again.

And again. This time he lets the answerphone finish his message.

LIAM: Everything I just said – pretend I didn't. Can we? Course we can be friends. That's all I want, really, just – to be with you. And then if anything happens, as and when you know – that's just a bonus. Yeah a brilliant bonus, like the bonus ball that makes the difference between a couple of grand and like a genuinely life changing sum of money – but still, you'd be an idiot to say no to that couple of grand. And I am not an idiot. Any more. I was, for a second, but that can happen, can't it? You can be an idiot for a bit and then drop it and just be normal again. So just please pick up, please?

He ends the call.

LIAM: Shit…

Noise at the door. LIAM's hopes rise – but then RICK and SUZE bundle into the room. SUZE carrying a big bag of chips, RICK carrying a couple of six-packs of cans.

RICK: Well with a bucket like yours you probably do prefer it sideways –

SUZE: Vile…

SUZE looks round.

SUZE: Where's your little friend?

LIAM: Dunno.

RICK moves into the room; puts down his six-packs. Pulls free a can and opens it. Takes drink.

LIAM: So I told her, like you said.

He's talking to RICK. RICK says nothing.

SUZE: And?

LIAM: And what d'you think?

SUZE: She didn't go for it.

LIAM: Not really no.

RICK drinks. LIAM's looking at him.

RICK: So what you fuckin looking at me for?

LIAM: You told me / that if I

RICK: *(Over him.)* You didn't have to listen.

LIAM: And that's all you got to say?

RICK shrugs.

SUZE: C'mon on love, plenty other fish in the sea.

LIAM: Oh really? Oh are there? What a devastating insight that is. I feel loads better now.

SUZE: You can't make somebody like you, and maybe she just didn't. She's young, you know. That age, they see some rugby lad with thighs like concrete and that's all they can see. It's her loss.

LIAM: Doesn't feel like her loss…

SUZE: Well, not now, no, but in time...

LIAM: Oh fuck off will you...

SUZE: *(Calm.)* You fuck off yourself you little shit.

LIAM looks at her.

SUZE: Oh yeah, he likes to chuck the swears about, doesn't like it so much when they start coming back...

LIAM sits down somewhere so he's not looking at .

SUZE gets on with eating.

RICK: Want some chips?

LIAM: Eff off with your chips.

RICK moves a little closer to LIAM.

RICK: The thing is, with girls –

LIAM: More wisdom is it.

RICK: Say when Doctor Who, is trying to stop the Daleks.

LIAM looks over at him, but doesn't speak.

RICK: And like the first thing he tries, doesn't work. So what then? Does he sit and sulk? Or does he / try something –

LIAM: *(Interrupting.)* Are you trying to use Doctor Who as a teaching tool for my romantic life?

RICK: I'm saying, does Doctor Who give up, at the first knock back?

LIAM: No he doesn't.

RICK: No he doesn't. Doctor Who keeps / on going.

LIAM: Please stop it now–

RICK: What?

LIAM: *(Beat.)* 'Doctor Who' is the show. The character is 'The Doctor'.

RICK: What's the fuckin difference?

LIAM: The damage it does my head hearing you say it wrong.

SUZE: Leave him stew, Vile.

LIAM: Yeah, leave me, why don't you.

Rick hesitates.

RICK: What I'm saying is, don't give up.

LIAM: So I have another go with Jen then and / what?

RICK: No no no no.

LIAM: No?

RICK: No, fuckin Jen's gone mate. You blew it. Forget her. She's like... *the Doctor's –*

He pauses, expecting congratulations for getting it right. LIAM is stony-faced.

RICK: – first plan. Now you need another plan.

LIAM: When you say, another plan, you mean –

RICK: Well like what other girls do you like?

LIAM: None.

RICK: None?

Liam shakes his head.

SUZE: Aw well there we are then.

RICK: So all the girls, your school –

LIAM: College.

RICK: – if they all tipped up here offering to shag you now – you'd send them on their way? Couldn't bear to stick it in even one of them?

LIAM: That's my standard? A girl I could bear to stick it in?

SUZE: Don't knock a good shag, Liam. Things grow from a good shag.

LIAM: Is that what you think, Suze? Explains a lot...

RICK: Hey. Cool it.

LIAM: Or what?

SUZE: Vile.

RICK: Bit of fuckin respect's all it takes.

SUZE: *Vile.*

> *RICK snaps out of it.*

SUZE: He didn't mean nothing. Alright?

> *RICK drinks, says nothing.*

LIAM: There's a girl called Emma. She's got this funny sort of... mouth but it's, you know. Cute.

SUZE: Alright, so what's this Emma into then?

LIAM: She's a bit... like she's not so full of herself as Jen? Like Jen's here slagging off her boyfriend to me: but in college she is a bit – oh, did I mention I'm going out with the captain of the rugby team?

RICK: Yeah her mum's a stuck-up bitch too.

SUZE: How d'you know her mum?

RICK: Got to know her years back. Couple of times. Not so much now...

SUZE: Jesus...

RICK: What?

> *SUZE turns away from RICK, back to LIAM.*

SUZE: Emma, she's a bit more down to earth?

LIAM: S'pose yeah.

RICK: Bit more your sort of level like?

LIAM: Fuck's that mean?

RICK: So, this Emma. Monday morning, you find your moment –

LIAM: She's not in Mondays.

RICK: Tuesday morning then. You find your moment, and you chat to her. Just anything. Just start it off. But you have to do it. Alright.

LIAM: Yeah, whatever.

RICK: You swear now. You'll talk to her when you see her next. And we take it from there.

LIAM: Alright.

RICK: We gotta plan, then. We're set. Tuesday morning, you're gonna talk to her. And we take it from there. And if doesn't work out with this Emma girl, we'll try the next one, and the next one, and –

There's a knock at the outside door.

RICK holds LIAM's gaze a second.

Then he walks to the front door. Opens it.

RICK: *(Off.)* Alright.

RICK walks back in. JEN follows him. Soaked.

RICK: Raining a bit then.

JEN: Little bit.

SUZE gets up, heads to the bathroom.

RICK: Yeah, was drizzling on us the way back from the chip shop.

JEN: Then it got a bit worse than that. I started walking and it pissed down so I called for a taxi and they said absolutely fucking nothing going, give it an hour an ring 'em again so I thought –

RICK: Come back wait here.

JEN: Yeah, if you don't mind?

RICK: We don't mind at all, do we? Do we, Lee?

LIAM doesn't answer.

SUZE is back with a towel.

SUZE: There you go love.

JEN: Aw cheers.

SUZE: You're drenched, look at you.

JEN: Did piss down on me slightly.

RICK: She wants to wait for her taxi.

SUZE: Yeah, course you can.

RICK: Yeah I said.

SUZE: You can't wait in these though, you're soaked. I'd give you something of mine but Vile's a bit funny about me leaving stuff here.

JEN: I'll be fine.

RICK: Liam'll dig you out something of his. Lee?

JEN: I'm fine I am.

RICK: See what you can find for Jen. Clean, mind.

LIAM: She says she's fine.

RICK: Do's you're fuckin told for once, will you.

LIAM heads off to his bedroom.

JEN: Honestly, taxi'll be here in a bit.

RICK: Taxi? But we got you chips.

SUZE: Yeah, stay and have chips.

RICK: I thought you were staying so I got extra.

JEN: That's really nice of you. Although I did say I wasn't…

RICK: Just in case.

SUZE: You head home now they'll only go to waste.

JEN: Yeah. I would…

LIAM return with a shirt and tracksuit bottoms.

He offers them to JEN, without a word.

JEN: Just I get the feeling maybe someone doesn't want me.

SUZE: Liam'd love to have you. For tea.

SUZE absolutely means the double-entrendre implied by the pause between 'have you' and 'For tea', and LIAM knows she does. He gives her a look.

JEN: Or I could just go.

LIAM shrugs.

JEN looks at him, not sure what to do.

SUZE: Liam.

LIAM: Was you went running off.

RICK: Go on, stay for chips. Sod the taxi I'll run you home after.

JEN: I could give you some money for petrol?

RICK: *(Smiles.)* No, you're alright.

JEN: Aw thanks, that's really good of you.

SUZE: D'you wanna get out of those wet clothes love?

JEN: Please. *(To LIAM.)* Can I use your room? Again.

LIAM: Yeah, use what you like. Again.

JEN hears the dig, goes.

RICK waits till JEN is safely gone.

RICK: What'd I tell you?

LIAM: I dunno, most of the time I'm not really listening.

RICK: She stropped off trying to get you to back down. You stood your ground. And you won.

LIAM takes this on.

SUZE: Oi, shall we eat off plates, if we got a visitor?

RICK: Yeah, they're in the kitchen.

SUZE: I know where they fuckin are you twat, come and give me a hand.

RICK begins to move, after SUZE.

RICK: She's up for it. Only thing is, have you got the balls?

RICK leaves to the kitchen, after SUZE.

And left alone, LIAM allows himself to think that maybe, just maybe, he is genuinely in with a chance with JEN.

And then there's the noise of JEN returning from his bedroom and LIAM locks all those sorts of thoughts down.

JEN enters.

Smiles at him. He smiles back.

She sits near him.

JEN: Listen.

LIAM makes a showing of giving her his full attention. It knocks her off-course a bit.

JEN: Listen.

She doesn't know what to say.

LIAM: I thought there was more to come after that.

JEN: Yeah so did I.

They smile at each other.

JEN: Look.

LIAM: I'm listening, I'm looking, what do I sniff you next?

JEN: I knew you liked me. I knew when we started talking about going to Regenerations, and…I said yes. Because I quite liked the idea that you liked me.

She falls silent.

JEN: And I think about it and I can't see me being with Jordan in like a year's time. So I think…finish with him then.

LIAM: Yes, definitely, you absolutely should.

JEN: But it's just…

LIAM: He's captain of the rugby team and…

JEN: Yeah I am actually that shallow…

SUZE and RICK return with plates and cutlery and things.

SUZE: *(To LIAM.)* You don't like their veggie burgers, do you?

LIAM: It's not about like, it's about they're cooked on the same grill as the meat –

SUZE: Which is why I didn't get you any. So it's cheese and chips for you. Jen, I don't know what you like, but I'm guessing you can't be as much of a fussy bugger's this lot so I got large of everything and there's bound to be something you can have.

RICK starts unwrapping the parcels of chips. Throughout the next section, the actors can interrupt the scripted dialogue with requests for salt, vinegar, etc.

RICK: These are mine, are they?

SUZE: Reckon so. Get stuck in, love.

JEN: I will. Whiff of chips and I'm starving.

RICK: You wanna beer Jen?

JEN grabs a plate, loads some chips on.

JEN: Ah... alright then, yeah.

RICK: There you go. Don't tell your mum.

JEN: Cheers.

LIAM is obviously expecting to be offered a beer. None comes his way.

LIAM: Am I getting one?

RICK: You're underage.

LIAM: Can I have a beer please.

RICK: You'll get all silly and embarrass yourself.

SUZE: Give him one, Vile.

RICK hands over a beer. Watches LIAM as he opens it.

SUZE: Gotta say, these are bloody good chips.

RICK: Fresh on, he said. You can tell. End of the night they're all soggy. But then end of the night who gives a shit.

SUZE: Never's good though, are they, as years ago.

RICK: No, I know what you mean.

SUZE: The taste, is like different?

LIAM: It's the fat. They used to fry chips in animal fat. Not any more.

SUZE: Is it?

LIAM nods as he eats.

LIAM: So they're like six percent less heart-attacky than they were.

SUZE: When I was little, it used to be a treat we had fish and chips every Saturday tea, only I'd have chicken cos I didn't like the bones. And I used to stuff 'em down me and get hiccups and heartburn...

RICK: Greedy mare.

SUZE: No, it was cos um…

She so obviously dries up that people look.

RICK: What?

SUZE: I don't wanna say.

She's not frightened, more embarrassed.

RICK: *(Beat.)* Oh okay. Suze doesn't wanna say. She's led us in, but now she doesn't wanna say so let's talk about / something else –

SUZE: If I didn't eat 'em quick I'd be too scared to eat anything. Cos it was tea time. Saturday. In front of the telly.

LIAM puts it together first.

LIAM: *You* watched *Dr Who*?

SUZE: Well it was on wasn't it? And I'd be cwtched into my dad crapping myself…

LIAM: *(A chant.)* One of us, one of us…

JEN: 'S alright Suze, girls are allowed to be geeks nowadays.

SUZE: Is it?

JEN: No, not really. But we're working on it.

LIAM: So which Doctor was yours then?

SUZE: Well I dunno who they are do I.

LIAM: Well was it in black and white, / or…

SUZE: *(Cutting in.)* How fuckin old d'you think I am?

LIAM: I wouldn't even dare / begin to…

SUZE: *(Cutting in.)* It was the one with all the hair.

LIAM/JEN: Tom Baker.

SUZE: And he was proper scary, not like today where they're all cuddly and they snog. Chuck us the red sauce, Vile.

RICK passes her the ketchup.

SUZE: You want some more love?

JEN: I shouldn't…Christ I sound like my mum!

SUZE: Go on, help yourself.

JEN: I was gonna say, I remember having chips when we were little, cos mum'd always be on these stupid diets? Like black coffee and grapefruit?

SUZE: Christ I remember that one…

JEN: And all you would eat was –

SUZE: – black coffee and grapefruit!

JEN: And end of the day, she'd be in a foul mood, surprisingly.

RICK: *(To LIAM.)* All as daft as each other.

JEN: So like seven eight o'clock she'd give up, she'd have to eat. But to stick to the diet, she'd have nothing in the house. Like literally nothing. Spices and… out of date icing sugar. So she'd be stamping round the place waiting for Dad to come home to send him out for chips.

RICK: Why didn't she go out for chips?

SUZE: She had the kids didn't she.

JEN: No it was like – it was one of her things. She got funny going out at night?

RICK: Bit of a, tense lady your mum?

JEN: Used to be. Chilled out a lot now. Since she discovered pinot grigio comes in boxes.

RICK: You know what I remember? The test card. See you haven't got a clue what that is.

LIAM: Of course we do, it's on the net – like everything.

RICK: I remember seven eight, I hated school. And I hated dinners the worst dunno why.

SUZE: Cos they were so shit.

RICK: Probably yeah. And one day, going into the hall, Miss Williams grabs me. And I'm thinking, what've I done now? – and she says your dad's here. And he was. And he took me out of school, for my dinner. I didn't even know you could do that – but you could. And I remember – walking, holding his hand, walking down the high street, thinking all my friends stuck in school, and me out with my dad. And we went to the chip shop. I had chips and battered sausage. And in the chip shop there was a telly, and I wanted the telly on and they said there was nothing on, but Dad made them put it on anyway. And it was just the test card. Only then they kept it on for the music. *(Eats a chip.)* I was what five? And one second I'm in school hating it – and the next I'm having chips with my dad. Like magic. And he did it the next day. And the next day. Every day that week. *(Beat.)* And then the next week he moved out. And I hardly saw him after that.

RICK eats. A little silence.

SUZE: He was saying goodbye.

RICK looks at her. Smiles. Picks up his drink.

RICK: Cheers everyone.

SUZE and JEN raise their drinks in response.

SUZE: I wish I'd known him.

RICK: He was a prick he was.

RICK has said this and meant it: he doesn't now.

LIAM is looking at him. RICK notices. Holds LIAM's gaze. Not challenging, for once. Just not looking away.

Finally LIAM breaks it.

SUZE: Stuffed. You wanna finish these for me Vile?

RICK: Aye go on.

JEN: Why'd you call him that? Vile.

SUZE: It's like a nickname.

JEN: What, cos he's – vile?

RICK: I look vile to you?

SUZE: Don't tempt her, she's trying to be polite.

RICK: If you're trying so hard the effort shows, you might's well not bother.

SUZE: It's cos… when he was younger, like, he used to get into scrapes. Like a lot.

JEN: When you say scrapes?

SUZE: Like pub on a Saturday night. Or a Friday night. Or a Thursday night…

JEN: But scrapes, though: what, is that, exactly?

SUZE: Like silly stuff. You look at my bird, sort of thing.

JEN: D'you mean, fights?

SUZE: You know, like boys do.

LIAM: I don't.

RICK: I have never started a fight in my life. *(Beat.)* Finished a few though…

JEN: So he's called Vile cos…

SUZE: Like you get called by what you do. So Dai the Butcher, Steve the Post. And they called him – Violence.

JEN: Oh okay.

SUZE: As a joke.

JEN: Course.

SUZE: This is all donkey's years now. He's calmed down a lot. Haven't you?

RICK: You put that beer away Jen.

JEN: Did I? Christ I did.

RICK: It's the salt innit. Salt gives you a thirst. Have another.

SUZE: I was saying it's years ago, Vile. All that stuff. You haven't smacked anyone for ages.

RICK: Christ no. *(Beat.)* Apart from that retard I broke his jaw.

SUZE had not simply forgotten that incident.

SUZE: Well yeah. Apart from him.

RICK: Cos that was what, less than a twelvemonth?

SUZE: Yeah but I thought not to mention that –

LIAM: What was this?

SUZE: – not wanting to scare the girl, like?

RICK: No, fair play, but – truth's the truth. And I'm not ashamed of it. Plenty of the stuff I done when I was younger, yeah, I was a fucking cock. But not that. That needed doing.

JEN: Sorry what?

SUZE: What it was – you know the York? You know how it gets Friday Saturday night?

JEN: Rammed.

SUZE: And you know what happens?

LIAM: What?

SUZE: You dunno: she does. What happens, in the York, when it's rammed?

But JEN doesn't know.

SUZE: If you're a girl.

Instantly she does.

JEN: You get felt up.

SUZE: And a grope of the arse – well whatever you know. But there was this bloke. Nathan. And he's a bit – simple, like.

LIAM: You mean he's got learning difficulties?

SUZE: That sorta thing, yeah. And people'd had a word, but it didn't go in? I think, cos of the – learning difficulties? He didn't get it. So I'm in there one night, go to the bar – and he's behind me. Goes under my skirt. Rams his fingers, right up in me. And like I say I'm not the first. And they chuck him out and he's just giggling? So Vile goes out there and –

LIAM: And what?

RICK: Hit him.

JEN: And broke his jaw.

RICK: I didn't mean to.

JEN: Still you must've hit him pretty fucking hard to do that.

RICK: I meant to hit him pretty fucking hard. I meant to hit him hard enough it would hurt, for a long time.

SUZE: And – I know, I do – but the fact is he's not been in there since. Not touched anybody. Nothing.

LIAM: So he's learned his lesson then?

RICK: Looks like it, yeah.

JEN: Didn't think to go to the police?

SUZE: Has anybody ever stuck their hand up you?

JEN: *(Beat.)* Fucking obviously.

LIAM looks: that this is obvious is a surprise.

SUZE: You go the police?

JEN shakes her head.

SUZE: Yeah exactly. And people'd told him. His mum and dad, had told him. His brothers, had told him.

JEN: Yeah, well...

SUZE: What, I should just put up with it, should I?

JEN: I'm saying, there's ways.

SUZE: There weren't. And some of the girls he was going after were young. Really young, like fifteen.

JEN: What were they doing in the York then, they're that young?

RICK: And you were never in there that age...

JEN: You broke the jaw, of a man with learning difficulties. That is fucking psychotic.

RICK: Fair enough. I get why you don't like it. But I'll tell you this. Week after, the kid's dad comes round. And you know what he says to me?

They don't.

51

RICK: He says, thank you, Rick. He fucking *thanks* me. Cos he says, his boy's learned now. Says if he'd carried on the way he was going, he'd've ended up in jail. And what the fuck do you think happens to some simple little kid in jail? You think he has it easy? I wouldn't think so. I wouldn't think so at all. But that's where he was headed. Till I stopped him.

JEN: Yeah, well –

RICK: The dad says, he actually says to me, by rights he should've done it himself. And I get that. Your own son – you're fucking soft. So fine. You think I'm a bit of a cunt fair play. I'm not saying it's a nice thing I did. I'm not saying it's good. But the kid keeps to himself these days, no trouble to anybody. And his own dad, shakes my hand. *(Beat.)* But what the fuck, you got more exams'n I'll ever have, you know best.

JEN: Yeah well.

The fight goes out of her a little.

JEN: It's just fucking tragic that's how it is.

RICK: No fucking disagreement from me, love.

She relaxes.

RICK: So. Another beer?

JEN: Yeah…no I might be off.

SUZE: Aw is it? You don't have to.

JEN: No, I'm not being – look, I'm sorry alright, I still don't like it, what you did –

RICK: I don't like it.

JEN: – but, Christ, what the fuck're you supposed to do?

SUZE: Fucking put up with it, is what you're supposed to do…

JEN: S'pose yeah.

RICK: And you shouldn't have to.

JEN: No, course. It's just it's getting a bit, late, you know.

RICK: No worries, I said I'd give you a lift. Gimme till I've finished –

He stops.

RICK: I can't can I?

SUZE: What d'you mean you can't?

He's got a beer in his hand.

RICK: This is what my…

SUZE: Third?

RICK: Fifth now, if that. Christ, I'm sorry love.

JEN: That's alright. What now?

JEN hasn't quite understood.

RICK: Well I'll be over won't I. For driving you home.

JEN: Oh.

RICK: Yeah. Sorry, I didn't think –

JEN: No, that's alright –

RICK: – like cos for myself I bomb round the lanes all sorts of states and I know I'm safe but, passenger in the car – different thing, see.

JEN: 'S alright, I'll ring the taxi again.

JEN phones for a taxi. Waits for the number to answer.

SUZE: Where you live love?

JEN: Maesteg Road?

SUZE: Christ that is a way.

The number answers. JEN asks for a taxi to Maesteg Road.

RICK peers at SUZE's plate.

RICK: You eating that?

SUZE: Does it look like I am?

RICK: You might be having a break.

JEN: Okay thank you.

Ends the call.

JEN: They only got two cars out this way and one of them just crashed.

SUZE: What about your mum?

JEN: She's funny driving at night.

SUZE: And there's no buses that way are there?

JEN: Christ no. Though once Prince William came and they re-routed everything so they did go –

She stops.

JEN: No basically.

SUZE: What we gonna do then?

JEN:'S alright. I'll walk.

SUZE: You'll get soaked.

JEN: I'll live.

SUZE: Late to be out walking alone.

LIAM: I'll come with.

JEN: I can't let you do that, it's miles. And raining.

LIAM: I don't know how you could stop me.

JEN: Break your legs?

RICK: Course. You know what you could do.

RICK waits till he has everyone's attention.

RICK: You could just crash here the night?

JEN: Well I –

RICK: If you're sure I'm not fucking psychotic!

He's making a point of being jovial.

JEN: Yeah alright fair play, I did go off on you a bit.

She looks to LIAM.

LIAM: I mean…if you want, whatever.

JEN: Whatever?

SUZE senses there is a negotiation that needs privacy.

SUZE: Gimme a hand clearing the plates, Vile.

RICK: You eat out the paper, it tastes better and you got fuck all to clear away.

SUZE: It's not fair is it – all the things people ask of you…

RICK follows SUZE off. JEN takes a moment to find what to say.

JEN: It's not that I don't want to stay.

LIAM: Right.

JEN: I mean…I could.

LIAM: Then definitely do!

JEN: It's just Jordan isn't it. Cos I haven't, like *officially* told him.

LIAM: But you are going to.

She doesn't say anything.

LIAM: Aren't you?

JEN: You know I am. *(Off his look.)* And don't look all chuffed with yourself, it's gonna break his fucking heart.

LIAM: No, I know. I'm sad for him, he seems like an alright bloke.

JEN: He is. As far as he goes.

A pause between them. LIAM fears to push the point might generate resistance.

LIAM: Does that really happen all the time?

JEN: …any sort of context?

LIAM: You get felt up in the pub.

JEN: Not *every* single time…

LIAM: Jesus Christ…

JEN: It's a tricky one cos – you wear jeans, you have at least got the protection of the thicker material but it means they can go straight in between the legs. You go with a skirt, they have to reach under it and then back up to get to your crotch which is a bit awkward, so they'll probably just

make do with a knead of the arsecheek – but then if they
do make the effort to get under and up and between, then
you'll actually feel the fingernails scrape down the lips of
your vagina.

LIAM: Jesus fucking Christ…

JEN: It's not super-fun.

LIAM: Someone should do something.

JEN: Yeah okay, what d'you think – petition? Awareness
raising meme on social media?

LIAM: I am really, really sorry, you have to put up with that
shit. On behalf of the male species.

JEN: Sometimes I feel like… there should be a fucking law
against it.

LIAM: There should, let's try that.

JEN: My mate Katie, she's in the York, it's rammed, she's
coming back from the bogs and – two fingers, right up her.
So she turns round and this bloke, is just grinning. With his
hand still, you know. And she's just had a-fucking-nough,
of putting up with it. So she slaps him. And this bloke,
takes his hand out of her crotch – and punches her in the
face. And she goes straight down. She's sat there in the spilt
beer, thick lip, bloody nose, people shoving past her. And
the bloke just slips off.

LIAM: They get him?

JEN: They what? And now every time some random even…
stares at her tits she's thinking where the fuck does this end
up? She wishes she'd let the fucker just get on with it. Cos
standing up to him just made everything worse.

LIAM: Seriously: how the fuck d'you cope with even going
there?

JEN shrugs.

JEN: Pre-drinks are a girl's best friend. Plus it's where everyone
goes. Where my mates go. Where Jordan goes…

LIAM: Is that where you're supposed to be going, tonight? Out with him to the York?

JEN: It is Saturday…

LIAM: I don't think you should. Cos it sounds horrible.

JEN: It really is…

She thinks about it.

JEN: That's it. I'm not going.

LIAM: And I'll be on the couch. Out here. You'll just be staying over. We don't have to do anything. If you don't want –

JEN: And you can calm it down too, I'm not staying here. I'm just gonna go home.

LIAM: Right. Okay.

JEN: Because I think – the first night we stay together, we should do it properly.

LIAM: Oh.

JEN: Not with me feeling all guilty about Jordan. So I'll go home. And tomorrow I'll finish with him. And then… you can whisk me away, in your magical blue box.

LIAM loves this idea.

But then –

LIAM: You know I haven't *really* got one, don't you?

SCENE TWO

LIAM in the living room. RICK enters.

RICK: Where's the lucky lady?

LIAM: Trying to talk her mum into coming picking her up. She said she didn't want me to hear her beg.

RICK: Reckon I could stand to hear her beg…

LIAM: That is… vile.

RICK: I can't believe I got her stuck here and you let her go. What is the point of you, honest to God…

LIAM: Yeah well actually, tomorrow she's going to see her boyfriend and finish with him.

RICK: So she says...

LIAM: So she will.

RICK: Or she might go see her boyfriend... trip and fall gob first on his cock.

LIAM: I don't know why I even bother listening / to you –

RICK: Well you might wanna start listening more. Cos what did I say would happen? I said you stand your ground, she'll come running back. And she fuckin did.

LIAM: She came back, to get out the rain.

RICK: You can get out the rain standing in a fucking bus stop. She didn't do that. She came back here.

LIAM doesn't answer.

RICK: I said she would: and I was right.

LIAM: Stopped clock.

RICK looks at him.

LIAM: Is right twice a / day.

RICK: Old fuckin joke.

RICK moves, to get another beer. This puts him standing behind where LIAM is sitting.

LIAM: I think it's an aphorism more than a joke. Is that what an aphorism is?

LIAM's talking to himself.

RICK: How'd I fuckin know?

LIAM's getting out his phone, to look up 'aphorism'

LIAM: And, in a million years, why'd I be asking you?

RICK watches him.

LIAM finds something.

LIAM: Ah right. Maybe technically just a proverb.

RICK: Is it.

LIAM: Cos you were on tenterhooks, weren't you, to find out.

LIAM gets back to his phone, diverted by something else.

RICK watches him a little while.

RICK: So why then?

LIAM looks at him, not following?

RICK: Why's it a proverb, not a – whatcha/call

LIAM: *(Cutting in.)* An aphorism?

RICK: Yeah.

LIAM: D'you actually care.

RICK: I wanna know.

LIAM: How would it ever be of use to you?

RICK: I wanna know.

LIAM: A proverb is a saying, like any saying that's being around forever. An aphorism, it'd have to be something you made up yourself. Like, not something / you'd heard someone else –

RICK: *(Cutting in.)* No I get it.

LIAM gets back to his phone.

RICK: Clever little fucker aren't you. Knowing the difference.

LIAM: I just read it on my phone?

To which he returns, again.

RICK: No, you've done well with her though. Jen.

RICK gets the beer. Opens it. Takes a drink.

LIAM: Christ well your approval is, the *only* thing, really, I care about.

LIAM doesn't even look up.

RICK moves across the room, nearer LIAM. Finds something to fiddle with.

RICK: That girl had her kid next door?

LIAM: Fuck do I know.

RICK: Just asking.

Drinks.

Watching LIAM.

And then he reaches out, tousles LIAM's hair.

LIAM recoils.

LIAM: Get, the fuck off.

RICK: Just seeing what you got on your hair.

LIAM: Nothing.

RICK: Fucking greasy then. She'll get fucking acne running her hands through that.

LIAM: Piss off.

RICK: Joking mun.

LIAM: And how, is it funny?

RICK moves away.

RICK: Keep thinking I can hear a baby crying. Like, off, you know.

LIAM doesn't follow.

RICK: So I reckon she has had it: next door.

LIAM: Oh, d'you know what that is?

RICK: What?

LIAM: No cos I hear that.

RICK: At night like.

LIAM: All sorts of times. It's – you don't mind me saying?

RICK: How would I mind?

LIAM: I'm just trying to think how to put it.

RICK: Simplest's best.

LIAM: Yeah, absolutely, so, in the simplest possible terms: it's after you've fucked Suze?

He lets it hang a second.

LIAM: Cos afterwards, she goes off and has a little cry? I say little cry…she locks herself in the bog and screams a good five ten minutes?

RICK: Har-de-fuckin-har.

LIAM: Really not joking.

RICK drinks again.

RICK: All I'm saying is, I'm glad you got a girl round cos, I was ninety per cent you were a poof.

LIAM: Is that the best you've got? Because – in that case I definitely am a poof. If that's what was worrying you. I'm the biggest poof this valley's ever seen. I'm a massive cockingsucking poof. Even bigger… than your mate Trev. Because he is. Oh he is. No doubt about it.

LIAM smiles.

LIAM: 'Poof'. Seriously. Do you do that –

LIAM makes the limp-wristed, Larry Grayson gesture.

LIAM: When you think someone might be gay? Do you?

RICK: Showing off a bit.

LIAM: Who'm I showing off to?

RICK shrugs.

RICK: It's what kids do. Show how big they are.

LIAM: How the fuck'd you know what kids do?

RICK: Cocky now cos you got your girl round.

LIAM: Or maybe now I know I definitely definitely am a poof, now that nagging doubt about my sexuality's been dealt with, I just feel more confident, more assertive.

RICK: Think you can say what the fuck you like and there's no come back.

LIAM: I *can* say what the fuck I like.

RICK: Is it.

LIAM: I'm not scared of you.

RICK smiles.

LIAM: Alright. I am. I am scared.

RICK: Oh I know that.

LIAM: You proud of yourself? That a boy is scared of you?

RICK: You got no reason to be.

LIAM: Oh really. None at all.

RICK: Okay. I get wound up, I might *say* I'll chuck you out, but it's / pissed talk –

LIAM: Chuck me out?

RICK: But I'd never. This is your home.

LIAM doesn't answer immediately.

LIAM: Aw well, there we go.

RICK: What then?

LIAM looks at him.

RICK: What?

LIAM: Chuck me out. *That's* what I'm afraid of?

RICK doesn't answer immediately.

RICK: You see you're good with words. And that's fine. Lot of the time you can talk your way out of trouble. But's a bad thing too. Cos you think you're safe with words. You think you can say what you like. And you can't. There are some things, you say them, you're in a heap of shit. *(Beat.)* Course if I'd brought you up, you'd know that.

LIAM: If you'd brought me up I'd've fucking killed myself by now.

RICK doesn't answer.

LIAM: Because she told me, before she went. What kind of bloke you are.

RICK: And what kind's that?

LIAM: I know why she ran away from you.

RICK: And she says it so it's true? Two sides to every story.

LIAM: Hers, yours. I know what I believe.

RICK: Course you do. Woman that ran off with you, never let me see you, never let me speak to you – course you believe her.

LIAM: I know what you are.

RICK: What?

LIAM doesn't speak.

RICK: You can't even fuckin say. Look at you. Mummy's boy.

LIAM: Well I had to be.

RICK: You turn up, and what do I do? Put a roof over your head, feed you. And who the fuck are you to me? Some kid I never met, that some pisshead says was mine. But in you come. And like that, this is your home. And where else you got would do that for you?

LIAM: Nowhere –

RICK: Exactly.

LIAM: – or I'd already be there.

RICK: Aw, clever.

LIAM: Not really.

RICK: I say your mum was a pisshead. She'd come home she wouldn't have a clue, where she'd been, what she'd been doing. So you could be mine. You could be half the blokes in town. Not just cos she was a fuckin slag. But she'd be out cold in the corner of the pub, anyone could've done anything, she'd never've had a fuckin clue. Except they knew fuckin better than to touch my girl.

LIAM: Wasn't she lucky you were there to look after her.

RICK: Aye, she fuckin was.

LIAM: Shall we actually get a DNA test done?

RICK: Fuck it why not.

LIAM: And then if I'm not yours, you can kick me out.

RICK: Suit me.

LIAM: Alright.

LIAM gets out his phone.

RICK drinks.

LIAM finds what he was looking for on his phone.

LIAM: Here we are. Ninety-nine quid. They send us swabs. We send 'em back special delivery, get the result the next day. I'll fill out the form, shall I?

RICK: If you want.

LIAM: Brilliant.

LIAM starts filling out a form on his phone.

RICK watches for a bit.

RICK: Oi.

LIAM: What?

RICK: Fuckin stop it.

LIAM's still filling out the form.

LIAM: Why?

RICK: Lee.

LIAM: Name's got two syllables. Just two. See if you can be arsed.

RICK: Liam. Joke's over, alright.

LIAM: Again: not joking. Tuesday… and we will know!

RICK: Fucked if I'm doing that.

LIAM: 'S alright. I'll wipe up your slobber when you pass out on the settee.

RICK: Gimme that phone.

LIAM: What, my phone? Don't think so.

RICK: Give it.

LIAM: Fuck off.

RICK snatches it off him.

LIAM: I'll just get it back when you're pissed.

RICK: You fuckin try it.

LIAM: I will.

> *RICK stares at him.*
>
> *LIAM grabs for the phone.*
>
> *RICK dumps the phone in a pint glass of water.*

LIAM: You prick.

RICK: I said stop.

LIAM: You absolute prick.

RICK: Now you'll know to listen.

LIAM: That was my phone.

RICK: And?

LIAM: Mum got me it.

> *RICK gets the phone out the glass.*

RICK: 'S probably alright.

LIAM: Just give it to me....

RICK: Was only in there two seconds –

> *LIAM grabs the phone off him, begins taking it to bits.*

LIAM: You got any rice?

RICK: Rice?

LIAM: As in pudding.

RICK: Why the fuck'd I have rice pudding?

> *LIAM grabs a tea towel, lays it flat on a surface.*

LIAM: No, the rice, I want the rice. Have you got any?

RICK: No.

LIAM: Course you fucking haven't.

RICK: What's the rice for?

LIMA's putting all the components of the phone out on the tea towel.

LIAM: Because if you put the parts of a wet phone in a bag with rice, the rice absorbs the moisture and saves your phone. Supposedly.

RICK: Shall I get some?

LIAM: It's probably bollocks. Sounds like bollocks.

RICK: There's a shop, they fix phones, we'll take it / round there.

LIAM: And what'll they do, in this shop?

RICK: There's bound to be something they can do.

LIAM: Yes there is: the thing I'm doing now.

RICK: They don't just fix phones, they sell 'em. Get you a new one if you want. Newer one than that.

LIAM: I don't want a newer one, I want mine.

RICK: Don't be like that mun.

LIAM: What'm I being like, Vile?

RICK: It's just a fucking phone.

LIAM: It's not just a fucking phone.

RICK: And I've said I'll buy you new. Don't be a cunt about it.

LIAM: Is that what I'm being?

RICK: Okay, sorry, but – Christ, mun…

LIAM stops his fiddling with the phone. Looks at RICK.

RICK: Well, you are.

LIAM: After they sent her home from the hospital. She looked like she was a two hundred years old, oxygen tanks and drips in her arm. I wanted to remember her. I wanted to remember the last time she was with me. And I knew she wouldn't want any pictures taken, with her in that state. So I waited till she was asleep. Snuck a few on this.

Beat.

LIAM: It was the last thing I had of her. The last thing I had. And now I've got nothing.

RICK: C'mon mun.

LIAM: C'mon what?

Not immediately –

RICK: You can't say you got nothing.

LIAM: What've I got then? Huh?

They stare at each other.

LIAM: What've I got, in the world?

RICK: You know.

And then LIAM folds up.

Begins to cry.

RICK: Aw now…

LIAM tries to lock it down –

– but then can't. Is crying properly.

RICK: You want Jen seeing you like this?

LIAM: Couldn't give a toss.

RICK: Aye well you should. No – one wants to fuck a crybaby.

LIAM cries.

RICK: Yeah alright give it a rest.

LIAM cries.

RICK: Liam.

LIAM cries.

RICK: We've heard enough.

LIAM: I fucking hate you.

RICK: Yeah we know.

LIAM cries.

RICK: This is just showing off. This is showing off, again.

LIAM: I'm going to my room.

RICK: No you are not. You are gonna sit there, and shape up.

LIAM tries to get past him.

RICK won't let him.

LIAM: The fuck are you doing.

RICK: You're gonna sit there, and we're gonna cheer you up, before Jen comes back.

LIAM: Piss off.

LIAM tries to shove past RICK.

RICK holds him back.

LIAM: What the fuck?

LIAM tries, with all his might, to get past RICK.

RICK can't hold him, has to shove him away. It's a hard shove. LIAM staggers back, and then falls. Hits his head. Cries out in pain and shock.

RICK: Now see?

LIAM's getting up.

RICK: Now look what you done.

LIAM's back on his feet. He's bleeding a bit.

RICK: You alright?

They look at each other.

Something in RICK breaks – he moves towards LIAM.

RICK: Listen, now, listen to me –

LIAM backs off.

RICK: No, I know, I know –

SUZE enters.

SUZE: What the fuck's going on?

RICK: Nothing.

She looks at LIAM.

SUZE: How'd you do that?

He doesn't answer, just looks at her.

SUZE: Your head's bleeding.

LIAM: Pigs come, at night, with teeth, but then I'm fine later.

SUZE: You what?

LIAM: After they go I'm fine.

SUZE: Liam, are you okay?

LIAM: I said I'm fine!

LIAM touches his head – finds the blood.

LIAM: Oh shit.

SCENE THREE

JEN and LIAM.

LIAM is blowing on the bits of phone with a hair dryer.

He stops.

LIAM: What d'you reckon?

JEN: Give it another while. Better safe than sorry.

She looks at him.

JEN: Has he done this before?

LIAM: Done what.

JEN: Hit you.

LIAM: He didn't hit me.

JEN: You look like you got hit.

LIAM: I hit my head.

JEN: When he shoved you.

LIAM doesn't respond.

JEN: Has he?

LIAM: No he has not hit me.

JEN: But.

LIAM: I didn't say but.

JEN: Really cos I definitely heard one.

LIAM: It's just when he's had a bit.

JEN: Lucky he only drinks birthdays and Christmas then.

LIAM: Not every time he drinks, obviously. Just he gets wound up.

JEN: And unwinding involves putting you bleeding on the floor.

LIAM: Just, once or twice, he's… pushed past me.

JEN: And once or twice is that literally one time, or two times, or does it mean more like half a dozen times.

LIAM shrugs.

JEN: You've been here *six months*.

LIAM: We're getting used to each other.

JEN: D'you think it's gonna get better? It is not gonna get better Liam. That is not how these things go. How they go is, they get worse. He's knocked you about once or twice and what happens? Fuck all. So that's normal now. Normal, for him, is pushing you about so hard you smash your head open –

LIAM: I didn't smash anything.

JEN: What would you prefer, then?

LIAM: I think you're being a bit melodramatic is all.

She stares at him. Not immediately –

LIAM: When he loses it with me, he feels like absolute shit afterwards. Only for about five minutes but still.

JEN: What?

LIAM: I piss him off on purpose. So he'll lose it. Cos it's funny how it torments him.

JEN: So it's your fault?

LIAM: Well, you know.

JEN shrugs. She doesn't.

LIAM: Yes. I make him do it. So it's my fault.

JEN: Or…maybe you're just saying that. Cos you're embarrassed. You're embarrassed, that your dad knocks you about. Because it makes you feel pathetic and weak

70

and you are, in the most non-stereotypical, twenty-first
century way, pretty keen on looking the big man in front
of me.

LIAM: Oh *that's* what I'm doing...

JEN: It's not you should be embarrassed. It's him. Jesus you
could've died...

LIAM smiles at her – come off it...

JEN: If you'd've hit your head a bit harder, / then Christ
knows –

LIAM: By that logic you could die any time you fall over.

JEN: You could.

LIAM: So best remain in a seated position at all times. In case
I die.

JEN: Is it happening more or less often, Liam.

LIAM doesn't answer.

JEN: He doesn't answer.

LIAM: I don't keep count.

She comes to a stop.

JEN: This is what you should be embarrassed about. This. It's
one thing him doing it, but you covering it up for him.

LIAM: There's nothing to / cover up –

JEN: Because that is actually a bit cowardly.

LIAM: I'm a coward am I?

JEN: I didn't say that.

LIAM: You just – obviously you just fucking did!

JEN: Alright, I'm sorry –

LIAM: My mum dies and I've got nowhere to go but this
shithole, with that cunt – and I'm a coward?

JEN: It was – I didn't mean it like that. I'm sorry.

They look at each other.

LIAM looks away.

LIAM: More often.

JEN: More often?

LIAM: Like the first month it was all – not exactly sweetness and light but – and then it was just he'd barge past me getting out of the room. Cos he couldn't stand my fucking whining any more. Then... you remember when I came into college with stitches?

JEN: You are fucking kidding me.

LIAM: He meant to just give me a tap. Just playful.

JEN: What'd you tell 'em in A&E?

LIAM: That I fell. Cos I was pissed. *(Beat.)* And a couple of times since then.

JEN: So it's just normal now.

LIAM nods.

JEN: What's gonna happen when you really piss him off? Cos he can't just give you a shove, or a tap. Cos that's every day. What's he gonna do, next time he's really angry?

LIAM: Playful headbutt. Playful kick to the crotch.

JEN: Playful broken bottle in your face...

LIAM: He does feel bad. After.

JEN: Course he does. He's not a monster. He's just a prick. *(Beat.)* And how do you feel?

He thinks about it, properly.

LIAM: Nothing that prick does is as hard as losing my mum, so...

JEN: But he could kill you, Liam. He could kill you put you in a wheelchair fuck knows.

LIAM: S'pose.

JEN: You suppose?

LIAM: I'll be careful.

JEN: You'll be careful? Fuck off...

LIAM: What then?

JEN: You'll get out.

LIAM: Get out to where?

JEN: Anywhere.

LIAM: Oh yeah sure, just, yeah, just go –

JEN: You cannot stay here.

LIAM: It's six more months. I finish the year, I'm off to uni, I never see him again.

JEN: If you make it six months.

LIAM: What'm I supposed to do? I've got nowhere to *go*.

JEN: Get your own place.

LIAM: Oh yeah, why didn't I think of that…

JEN: People do. At your age.

LIAM: Who has. Who do you know, has set up on their own?

JEN: But you could.

LIAM: So – walk into a job, do I? Cos that's a piece of piss. Then get myself a place. Then – oh hold on. When do I do my A-levels.

JEN: Do them part-time.

LIAM: Oh yeah. In the evening maybe. When I get home from work. That would be it.

JEN: I'm not saying it would be easy.

LIAM: Oh okay. Oh that's fine then. Oh so it'd be hard, but tough fucking luck. *(Beat.)* Could you do that?

She doesn't answer.

LIAM: Course you fuckin couldn't.

JEN: This is your life's at stake. You're gonna risk that, so you can finish your A-levels?

LIAM: I've got no choice.

JEN: Yes you have. Yes you bloody have. Just you're too scared to take it.

LIAM: That's nice. Thanks.

JEN: Fuck being nice. This is your *life*.

They look at each other.

JEN: If it was me. If it was my dad, hurting me, what would you say? Tell me to just chance it? Cos never know he might *not* put me in hospital?

LIAM: I'd tell you to get the fuck out.

JEN: Well then.

LIAM: But I don't think I'd call you a coward if you stayed.

She doesn't say anything.

LIAM: Cos that's fuckin harsh Jen.

JEN: D'you know what I think? I think, when you start going out with someone, you think they're the best thing ever. So you're super-nice to them. Much better than you are to yourself. But as it goes on, they get to be part of the furniture. Part of you. So if you're good to yourself, you're good to them.

They look at each other.

JEN: So I think, if we were together. In the end. What you put up with for yourself, you'd put up with for me.

LIAM: That's right, cos this is all about you…

JEN: I'm saying it cos, I think you're the kind of person, you care more about other people than you do yourself.

LIAM: Yeah, well…that's what it is, being half-decent isn't it.

JEN: And it's lovely, but – it gets to a point, if you put up with shit for yourself, the people who care about you have to put up with it too.

She gets up.

JEN: I'm gonna start off for home.

She gets her things together.

JEN: Hope your phone's alright.

LIAM: Me too.

JEN: Said you should've backed it up.

LIAM: Yes, I know.

JEN: But you didn't.

LIAM: Yes, I know.

JEN: Even though apparently it was super-important to you.

LIAM: No, that's nice. Have one last go, why not.

JEN looks at him: makes a decision.

JEN: You should come.

LIAM: …for a walk?

JEN: Leave here, right now, and come with me, to my house. We've got fuck all room but you could stay for a bit. Coupla weeks at least. Get yourself sorted somewhere. You could.

LIAM: And then what?

JEN: I don't know. We'll find something.

LIAM: So I've got a week, and then –

JEN: I don't know but it's got to be better than some prick who's gonna –

She falls silent. Noise off.

JEN: Come on.

LIAM: To what?

JEN: You and me now. Come *on*, mun.

She holds out her hand to him.

LIAM: I can't.

SUZE sticks her head round the door.

SUZE: We alright?

JEN: Super-alright thanks Suze.

SUZE: Yeah fair play. Now, I got a big old idiot of a bloke here, and he's feeling a bit of a twat to be honest.

Neither JEN nor LIAM speak.

SUZE: So's it alright he comes in or what?

LIAM: His place.

SUZE: *(To off.)* Come on then.

SUZE moves into the room. RICK shuffles after her.

SUZE: And?

RICK: He knows I'm sorry.

SUZE: Ah well that's fine then.

RICK: I'm sorry, alright.

JEN: Tell it to the police. That's right, we called them.

RICK: Where are they then?

JEN: *(Beat.)* There's a wait.

LIAM: We didn't call the police.

RICK: Call 'em if you want.

JEN: We could've. That's assault that is.

RICK: What was?

JEN: Look at him!

SUZE: Vile.

RICK: Listen, I don't wanna argue...

JEN: You shoved him so hard he fell over.

SUZE: Sorry Jen – were you there?

JEN: He told me.

SUZE: Right so you weren't.

JEN: He said it, I believe him.

SUZE: I believe him too: just, be nice to hear what *he* thinks happened.

SUZE is staying calm.

LIAM: He shoved me, didn't he.

SUZE: Are you sure?

LIAM: Sure I ended up on the floor.

SUZE: No, no one's saying you didn't. Are you sure, that's cos Vile shoved you?

JEN: Just tripped, did he? Floor a bit slippy?

SUZE: Listen. Jen. You're a nice girl but – I swear to God love.

Unsaid: if you don't shut up…

JEN: Oh that's lovely.

LIAM: Yes, he shoved me. Definitely.

SUZE: Is it?

LIAM: Yes.

SUZE: Cos that's not what Vile says. Is it Vile?

They look at him.

RICK: What'm I gonna say?

SUZE: Say what you said to me.

RICK: He knows what he thinks.

SUZE: Yeah, but…

RICK: And he thinks that? He thinks I'd fuckin…

RICK looks at LIAM till LIAM looks back at him.

RICK: I never would.

LIAM: How'd I end up on the floor then?

RICK: You got pissed off with me, and you were off, you were out the door, and I didn't get out your way fast enough, and you crashed into me and sort of1… bounced off.

SUZE: So you didn't shove him at all.

RICK: I put out my hands, to try to sort of, steady him like.

SUZE: So it might've looked –

RICK: – exactly yeah –

SUZE: – like you were shoving him. But you weren't. You were trying, to stop him falling.

RICK: Course.

JEN: And what about the time he needed stitches?

SUZE: He fell.

JEN: Falls a lot, doesn't he.

RICK: Now, that was my fault.

JEN: Well. At least you're not fucking lying about it.

RICK: I should never've given him them last two beers.

JEN: Sorry?

SUZE: Time he got stitches. He fell cos he was pissed.

RICK: If I'd known he'd been drinking out with his mates, I never would've given him those cans when he come home. Never.

JEN looks to LIAM.

JEN: *Were* you pissed?

LIAM: I'd had a bit, yeah.

JEN: You didn't say.

LIAM: And?

JEN: But it was him gave you the stitches? Not an accident?

LIAM: Well what I can remember…

SUZE: Yeah but – it is easy, to get confused. When things get a bit het up. Like've you ever been in a proper fight?

LIAM nods. This surprises SUZE.

SUZE: Have you?

LIAM: Have you seen the way I dress?

SUZE: Aye, fair play. Myself, what I find is, getting hit – it scrambles your brains a bit? And all your hormones are going? All your adrenaline? Sometimes things get a bit mixed up. I've had it. Did that girl bump into you just trying to squeeze past, or did she spill your drink deliberate? And when you're riled up the bitch did it on purpose. But actually, maybe…

LIAM: I'm not talking about a girl, I'm talking about / him –

SUZE: And when you've been drinking, of course, that hardly helps keep things straight in your head.

LIAM: I know what happened. He got angry, and he punched me, and I ended up getting stitches. And tonight he shoved me, and I ended up on the floor.

SUZE: Course you been drinking tonight as well.

LIAM: One beer!

SUZE: And there's no way, at all, it could've happened different? No way, that you might've just fell cos you were pissed? And then – remembered it wrong? That's actually impossible is it?

LIAM: I suppose it's not actually impossible.

SUZE: Alright okay. So it is possible, then.

LIAM: In theory yes.

SUZE: Right so it might be just accidents. All of it.

JEN: I can't fuckin believe this...

SUZE: *(Controlled.)* You know what love? You remind me of me. Cos I needed a fuckin slap when I was your age.

She turns back to LIAM.

SUZE: Cos I think you should think about what you're saying Lee. You're saying your dad hits you – that's fuckin serious stuff love.

LIAM: Well she thinks I should go. Before he puts me in hospital.

RICK looks to JEN.

JEN: Well he should.

SUZE: You're not wrong love. Course he should. If he's getting hit, he should run for his fucking life.

LIAM: So I'll be off then? Jen says I can stay at hers.

SUZE: Well that's very nice of your mum, Jen. The only thing I would say, is – what if there's been a bit of a mix-up. What if we're sending a boy away from his dad – cos of a mix-

up? Now, I wasn't there, when these things happened, / so
I don't know

LIAM: Yeah well I was, and / I do.

RICK: You haven't got a fucking clue boy. I might be fucking
raging with you. I might chuck things and punch the
walls. But I could never lay a hand on you. Cos if I did – I
couldn't fuckin live with myself. And you'll understand one
day. I never would've. But I do now. Once you got your
own child / then you –

LIAM: I am not your child.

RICK: No, fair play, you're a grown man, just about. I'm just /
saying –

LIAM: Mum said, when you found out she was pregnant, you
vanished. Didn't see you for weeks. And then you showed
up. You sat her down. And you had five hundred quid, in
twenties and tens. And you gave it to her. And you said,
there you go love. That's for you. To get rid of it.

JEN: Fuckin hell...

LIAM: Is that true?

RICK turns away, starts another drink.

LIAM: So I was never your child. And that was your choice.

JEN: What a fucking cunt.

RICK looks at her.

JEN loses her nerve a little.

RICK pulls out a can from the pack, offers it to her.

RICK: Sorry love, rude of me.

JEN shakes her head. RICK turns back to LIAM.

RICK: You do stupid things when you're young.

LIAM: Is it.

RICK nods.

LIAM: You say stupid it's coming across just fucking nasty.

RICK: Sometimes you start out stupid you end up being nasty.

LIAM: Can't quite see how that works myself.

RICK: Give you time.

A silence. Which SUZE breaks.

SUZE: What we're saying is, you might've got things wrong Liam. Maybe, in the mix-up, you thought / your dad had done things –

RICK: Give it a rest Suze.

SUZE: Sorry, sod me for trying to help.

RICK: Thing is. Maybe your girl's right.

LIAM: Right how.

RICK: I get a bit rough. When I've had a few. And there's always the chance. You could piss me off.

LIAM: What d'you mean?

RICK: Cos you haven't got the wit to know, have you, when you should keep it shut. You'll wind me up when I'm not in the mood. You haven't got a clue.

LIAM: Are you serious?

RICK: If I laid a finger on you, I couldn't live with myself. So perhaps best you should. You know.

LIAM: Have the balls to fuckin say it.

RICK: You should go.

LIAM: Go where, exactly?

RICK: She said you could stay at hers.

LIAM: For *a week.*

RICK: There's bound to be places.

LIAM: What places? What places do think there are?

RICK: Somebody'll take you.

LIAM: No they – why do think I came to you? Cos there was *nowhere else.*

RICK: You'll sort yourself out.

LIAM: I know there are some people, some people are off at sixteen, standing on their own two feet, and they cope. I'm not like that. I'll be on the streets.

RICK doesn't answer.

LIAM: And I'm not – no – one's gonna be scared of me, are they – on the streets They'll all go for me. I won't last a month.

RICK: The thing is, boy…

RICK stops.

RICK: I think you'd make it.

LIAM: Not a chance.

RICK: There's a bit of steel in you I reckon.

LIAM: Not really.

RICK: There is if you're my son.

LIAM: I know I'm a dick. I know I shoot my mouth off. I won't. I won't anymore. Whenever you've had a drink, then I'll button it. I won't wind you up.

RICK: No.

LIAM: Please.

RICK: No.

LIAM: I'll be good.

RICK: It's not about you being good. It's about not leaving you in harm's way. I'm sorry, son.

LIAM: Fuck you.

JEN: Come on Liam, let's go.

LIAM doesn't respond to her.

SUZE: You sure about this, Vile.

JEN: I'll help you pack, yeah.

LIAM: My mum dies. I have to go live with a prick in the middle of nowhere. And now – you can't keep your fists to yourself once you've had a drink – so I have to go. But why's it me? Why's it always me's got to do the hard thing? Why can't it be you? You're supposed to be the grown – up. So if you can't control yourself when you're pissed – stop fucking drinking. Stop it. Do that one thing. Or is that too hard for you?

RICK: I've had a drink every day since I was fourteen.

LIAM: So stop! Just for a few months, till I'm gone. Then drink yourself to fucking death for all I care.

RICK doesn't answer.

LIAM: I've never asked you anything. I'm asking you this.

Still doesn't answer.

LIAM: Can you do this. For me. Please.

And RICK realises –

RICK: Course I fucking can.

They stare at each other.

RICK: Right then.

RICK offers his can to SUZE.

RICK: You want that?

She takes it.

SUZE: You actually serious?

RICK's moving.

SUZE: Vile?

RICK's moving round the place, collecting cans and bottles on the table.

SUZE: You're not gonna chuck it all, are you?

RICK: If it's around, I'll drink it. There's a skip down the road.

RICK races round the place, into the kitchen.

SUZE: What, the fuck, have you done?

LIAM: I don't know.

RICK comes back with bottles of vodka and whisky, and a cardboard box, and a bag for life.

Starts putting the bottles into the box and bag.

RICK: Gimme a hand with this?

SUZE: 'S a fuck've a lot of booze to waste, Vile.

RICK: Yeah you're right. That's dull.

Moving slower, thinking, he finds a bottle of sherry and some odd liquer tucked in a cupboard. Adds them to the collection.

RICK: We'll take it all to the park. Leave it for the kids. They'll go fucking mental.

RICK picks up the box.

RICK: C'mon, you take them.

Indicates the bag to SUZE. Heads out.

SUZE takes the bag. Makes to go. Stops at the threshold.

SUZE: You know what your dad's like, sober?

LIAM: No.

SUZE: No. Me neither.

SUZE goes.

JEN: You think he's serious?

LIAM: Christ knows.

JEN: He looked pretty serious.

LIAM: He actually did.

JEN: And do you think it would make a difference? If he wasn't pissed the whole time.

LIAM: It is only when he's pissed he gets... lively.

JEN: That's a really, a thing. If he stops drinking.

LIAM: No I know.

They look at each other.

LIAM: Fucking *hell*.

JEN: Liam that's brilliant. You were brilliant.

LIAM: Well you know.

JEN: Aw come on mun you stood up to him. And not like in a shit stupid way that just made everything worse. You just told him what he needed to hear.

LIAM: And he *listened* is the thing.

JEN: Cos you made him.

A little silence.

JEN: Shall I get these back to you Monday?

He takes a moment to realise: the clothes.

LIAM: I suppose yeah.

She goes over. Stands near him. Kisses him on the forehead.

JEN: I'm really proud of you, you know.

They look at each other.

And then JEN turns away to go.

LIAM: Cos we've had a great day, haven't we.

JEN: Yeah, course.

LIAM: And then it got a little bit weird. And a little bit scary. And then something amazing happened. I stood up to him. And he backed down.

JEN: It was amazing.

LIAM: And it only happened, cos of you. Cos of you being here with me.

She doesn't say anything.

LIAM: And I think, we'll look back, and this will be the first day we were together. Because you are going to finish with Jordan. You know you are. And yeah sure this day could end with you trudging back across town in the rain. But I just think. Looking back. It'll just seem silly, that we didn't finish this amazing day, together. Just curled up, holding each other, till we drift off to sleep. Cos I don't know about you but I get so lonely, going to sleep on my own.

JEN: Yeah me too.

LIAM: Yeah so… don't.

She thinks about it.

Then puts down her bag.

SCENE FOUR

RICK and LIAM.

RICK: It was like – Willy Wonka in the chocolate factory. The kids couldn't fuckin believe it. Like half of them wouldn't touch it cos they thought there was something dodgy?

LIAM: I wonder why that would be...

RICK: They did though, in the end. One girl, just started necking the vodka, I had to say, cool head now love, you'll put yourself in harm's way.

LIAM: Incredibly responsible of you.

RICK: Fuck 'em, they don't have to drink it.

LIAM: But they will, and what if –

RICK: Here we fuckin go...

LIAM: – what if one of them falls down in the road gets run over?

RICK: 'S not gonna happen is it.

LIAM: It could.

RICK: Those kids are in that park getting hammered every weekend: they know what they're doing.

LIAM: Yeah, every weekend they don't have the entirety of your stash to work through.

RICK considers.

RICK: Ah, fuck 'em.

LIAM: Nice.

A little pause.

RICK: She's alright, your girl.

LIAM: She's not mine.

RICK: Not yet. In the bag though, isn't it.

LIAM: I mean, you don't talk about people as belonging to other people.

RICK: Fuck me is there nothing you can't make a fucking drag.

LIAM: Ask me again on my deathbed.

RICK: I tell you what I was thinking – I remember my mum trying to give up smoking. Christ she was a miserable bitch then. D'you reckon it's the same with drink?

LIAM: You've honestly never been a day without a drink? Since you were fourteen.

RICK: Maybe thirteen. Could be twelve.

LIAM: Like not if you were ill or something and you just didn't feel like it?

RICK: Never get ill.

LIAM: You were all last Sunday chucking up.

RICK: That was hungover not ill.

LIAM: You've really not had a day where you didn't touch a drop? Not one? Ever? In all these years?

RICK: Not even one.

LIAM stares at him.

RICK: I'm probably bullshitting a bit there.

LIAM: Oh really?

RICK smiles at him.

LIAM doesn't quite smile back.

RICK: And I don't mind, truth be told. Probably do me good in the end, and / it's only a couple of months –

LIAM: Would you maybe not mind making yourself scarce.

RICK: Why's 'at?

LIAM: Cos she's still here. She's staying over.

RICK: Bloody hell, how'd you get her to do that?

LIAM: I didn't get her to anything: she decided to.

RICK: 'S hope for you yet. Where is she then?

LIAM: Bathroom.

RICK: Getting ready for action…

LIAM: She's in my bed, I'm on the couch. Nothing's going to happen.

RICK: She wears a skirt size of a belt. *Decides* to stay over at yours. And now she's gonna peel her clothes off, climb into your filthy pit… and she doesn't want nothing to happen. Course not.

LIAM: Nothing's going to happen, because she hasn't finished with her boyfriend yet. Not officially. I mean she's gonna. Definitely.

RICK: Well…

LIAM: Well what?

RICK: You know what this is? This little night with you?

LIAM: I know whatever you think, I don't need to hear it.

RICK: Course, what do I know.

RICK moves. Without really thinking about it, looks in a cupboard. Finds a six-pack (of bitter: everything else he's drunk has been lager). Pulls off a can, opens it and begins to drink.

LIAM: What the fuck are you doing?

RICK: What'd you mean?

LIAM: The can.

RICK looks at the can.

Then realises.

RICK: Aw, fuck…

LIAM: What's that – not even half an hour.

RICK: It was a fuckin – force of habit. Look.

He puts the can down.

LIAM: Pathetic.

RICK: Alright.

RICK takes the can out to the kitchen.

Comes back.

RICK: Poured it away. Satisfied now?

LIAM: I thought you got rid of it all?

RICK: I thought I had! I just forgot about them, they were a Christmas present. From like fuckin... two thousand and nine. I don't even like the stuff. That's how come it's still here. Come on, mun. It was one slip.

LIAM: Within – ten seconds of swearing blind you're off it for good.

RICK: You never said for good, you said, for / a few months –

LIAM: *(Cutting in.)* You know what I fucking mean.

RICK: What, you think I'm not gonna do it?

LIAM: What d'you reckon?

RICK: You think you're not fuckin safe here, with me?

LIAM: I think...you haven't got a clue what it is, to do something for somebody else.

RICK: I let you into my fucking house!

LIAM: I bet Suze talked you into that.

RICK: Why, what's she said?

LIAM: I knew it!

RICK: Look. You think you're not safe? You are fuckin safer with me than you've ever been.

LIAM: Yeah I really feel it.

RICK: How many times've people picked on you, since you been here?

LIAM: Picked on me how?

RICK: Like, going round the place dressed like a fucking paedo. You said, at home, people'd shout at you, take the piss.

LIAM: Yeah course.

RICK: 'S that happen here?

LIAM: Get the odd look.

RICK: You get the odd look? You go about the place with a fucking fez and bow tie and tweed jacket even when it's fucking baking hot? I bet you get the odd fucking look. But how often, does someone shout at you, and call you a wanker?

LIAM: Once in Cardiff.

RICK: How many times *here*.

LIAM thinks about it.

LIAM: Actually... none.

RICK: And why's that d'you think?

LIAM: I dunno – I suppose I thought Dr Who's the only thing that's happened here in basically, forever, so – you know. People are grateful.

RICK looks at him, smiling.

LIAM: What then?

RICK: People know, you're my boy. And they know better than to lay a fucking finger on you.

LIAM takes this in.

RICK: See? You are safer here with me, than you have ever been.

RICK calms a little.

RICK: But like I'd ever get a word of thanks for it.

RICK waits for LIAM to respond. But he doesn't.

RICK: Right I'll be off to bed then.

LIAM: Alright, alright – what?

RICK: What'd you mean what?

LIAM: You were dying to tell me. What it is, this night. Jen staying here.

RICK looks at him.

LIAM: Or don't, I don't care.

But clearly he does care.

RICK: She's testing the goods. Seeing how it would be, to be with you, instead of him. And if you don't measure up – off she trots back to Jordan the rugby lad. This is your shot at glory boy. You blow it tonight, and it's game over.

LIAM: Thanks, that's making me feel great, and, um, suddenly very nervous about something that felt very natural and easy, so thank you.

RICK: So what you gotta do is, you gotta make it so she can't go back to him.

LIAM: Remind me how I control the actions of another human being, exactly?

RICK: Is she a slag?

LIAM looks at him.

LIAM: What d'you think I'm gonna say to that?

RICK: Yes she is, or no she isn't.

LIAM: I absolutely refuse, to define her on those terms –

RICK: Cos it's a bit of a slag move dossing down here at yours when she's with another bloke, but still, by the letter of the law, like, it's no foul. Cos you know. You're 'just mates'. So maybe, she isn't a slag. In her heart of hearts.

LIAM: Um…okay. She is not a slag.

RICK: You're in then, aren't you.

LIAM: How exactly?

RICK: A slag could fuck you, wetwipe round the gash on the way home, and be back shagging her boyfriend in the morning. Jen's not like that.

LIAM: I wouldn't have thought she was the… wetwipe round the gash type, no.

RICK: So something happens with you, she's not gonna be able to lie to him. She's not gonna be able to pretend.

She'll have to tell him. And that's it for her and Jordan.
He'll dump her like a busted fucking fridge.

LIAM takes this in.

RICK: So there's your answer. You close the deal tonight… and
that girl is yours for keeps.

SCENE FIVE

*LIAM sitting on the couch. If not in a sleeping bag then one draped over
him.*

*JEN comes in, face washed for bed. Wearing one of LIAM's T-shirts.
Massive on her.*

She has a toothbrush. It is pink.

JEN: Ta for the lend.

Offers him the toothbrush back.

LIAM: I generally keep it in the bathroom?

JEN: Yeah course.

He takes it.

JEN: It's pink.

LIAM: I know.

JEN: Deliberate choice.

LIAM: Smashing gender stereotypes everywhere I go. Even
first thing in the morning.

JEN: And last thing at night.

LIAM: And often in the middle of the day, if I've got a bit of a
manky mouth on.

They look at each other.

JEN: I'll be off to bed then.

LIAM: Enjoy it.

JEN: You'll be alright, on the settee.

LIAM: What's the worst that can happen?

JEN: *(Beat.)* You fall asleep with a lit cigarette, settee catches fire, you burn to death.

LIAM: I don't smoke.

JEN: Well it is very bad for your health. *(Beat.)* Jordan um, text me? When I was doing my teeth and everything.

LIAM: Oh yeah.

JEN: Asked where I was today?

LIAM: Okay.

JEN: And I am shit at lying.

LIAM: I don't believe you.

JEN: No, serious, I get all nervous and giggly.

LIAM: Even by text?

JEN: Absolutely yeah every text like a dozen giggly emoticons to sign off. Can't help myself.

LIAM: *(Beat.)* Say it then.

JEN: I told Jordan. Where I'd been, today. And who with. And um –

She pauses.

LIAM: Do not fucking X-Factor me Jen, I don't deserve that.

JEN: He was, completely not bothered.

LIAM: That's good, isn't it.

JEN: I thought, if he knew I was friends with you, he'd just be furious?

LIAM: Why?

JEN: Cos – obviously. You're so different to him. And me being friends with you is sort of saying…I wish he was different to how he is?

LIAM: No. It's saying, you want him, and maybe you thought you wanted me, and maybe you thought you had to make a choice: and now maybe you don't. You can keep him as boyfriend, and be friends with me. Best of both worlds.

JEN: No!

LIAM: It is though.

JEN: It just sounds fucking horrible when you put it like that.

LIAM: D'you think?

JEN: Makes me sound a horrible person.

LIAM: You're not a horrible person.

JEN: Thank you. Cos I think – we've got a real connection? And maybe I'm just not – maybe I'm just this stupid little teenage girl still and when I've grown up a bit, I really think, maybe, you and me might end up together, like in the long run. I know that sounds weird / saying it now –

LIAM: *(Cutting in.)* I don't think you're a stupid teenage girl at all.

JEN: Well you're very nice.

LIAM: I think… you're just out for as much as you can get. Like all humans.

JEN: D'you know, when I have guests at my house, I'm super-nice to them. Like if they fart, I blame it on the dog.

LIAM: You haven't got a dog.

JEN: That's the lengths I go to, I invent imaginary pets to avoid pointing out, my guests' failings.

LIAM: I've got a suggestion.

JEN: Okay.

LIAM: Why not have me as boyfriend, and be friends with Jordan? I wouldn't mind. I'm not the jealous type.

JEN: Yeah…

LIAM: Just think about. Try it out a week or two?

JEN: The problem would be – being friends with Jordan. What would that – what would that even *be?*

LIAM: It's mostly a physical thing, with you two.

JEN: He does try to talk to me sometimes. I just pick up my phone and look at… anything. And then after about twenty seconds so does he. *(Beat.)* Or in private I find him something better to do with his mouth.

She looks at him – he's not smiling.

JEN: Sorry.

LIAM: You say sorry. But know what you're doing, when you say things like that.

JEN: It was just a joke...

LIAM: You know what's happening in my head, don't you, when you say stuff like that.

JEN: And you quite like it. Don't / pretend you don't –

LIAM: *(Cutting in.)* Jen. Seriously. Get over yourself. If you scurry back to Jordan, it won't be the worst thing that's happened to me.

JEN: You sure? I'm quite a catch.

LIAM: It won't be the worst thing that's happened to me this year, even.

She looks at him.

JEN: Oh shit I'm so sorry...

LIAM: 'S alright.

JEN: It really is not.

LIAM: No. It's not. But what's wrong is not you forgetting about it. You forgetting about it is nice, actually.

JEN: It doesn't feel nice.

LIAM: Does to me. Feels like a relief. Like Rick. If he was less of a twat, he'd be asking about it all the time, or maybe occasionally, or ever. But he doesn't. He doesn't, ever, say a thing and actually – that's easiest.

JEN: So you don't think about it.

LIAM: I think about it all the time. I think – how long now till she comes through the door and takes me home?

JEN: Shit, Lee...

LIAM: You know you get pins and needles? Say in your leg. And you can't walk. But you don't really worry about it because, you know it'll go and you'll be fine in a minute? This is like that. I'm not worried cos, it'll be fine, in a minute.

They sit.

JEN: Was she nice?

LIAM looks at her. And then smiles.

JEN: I'm so sorry...

LIAM: Yeah cos like, if my mum died but she was a bitch, I wouldn't mind so much?

JEN: I'm a fucking idiot aren't I.

LIAM: She was nice. I mean, probably since I was thirteen I slightly thought she was a twat but, after getting the diagnosis and then the surgery and the chemo and then, when it became clear she was really going to die, I probably, some point in that process, started to see her good points, quite a lot more than I had.

JEN: Do you –

LIAM: No I don't miss her. Why would I miss her? She's coming to get me any second. Listen, that's her. Here she is –

And he points at the door.

LIAM: Now!

The door does not open.

LIAM: Or any time in the next ten minutes.

JEN: I'm trying to decide is it brave or weird you're sort of smiling about it the whole time.

LIAM: It is so, so brave.

JEN: I think it is.

LIAM: Which means you don't need to worry about me. Or feel guilty. Or make an effort to be nice, or do anything.

You definitely don't have to be with me, if actually you
want to be with your boyfriend.

JEN: Okay.

LIAM: Alright.

They look at each other.

LIAM: Alright then.

JEN: Night then, Liam.

He smiles.

And she turns away, reaches for the door –

– and as she turns, LIAM makes a decision.

LIAM: You know you're supposed to go through these stages.

JEN stops.

LIAM: When you know you're gonna die? Like… anger,
denial, pathetic last minute embrace of religion, then
acceptance.

JEN: I've never understood what that is.

LIAM: Acceptance?

JEN: Yeah.

LIAM: You accept you're gonna die.

JEN: That's it?

LIAM: Yeah.

JEN: I always thought it'd be more.

LIAM: More how?

JEN: Like… you know how if you believed in heaven? Really
believed? Then dying –

LIAM: Would not fucking worry you at all.

JEN: – because you weren't going to, really. I thought
when you 'accepted' you were going to die, something
happened, so it was like you felt you weren't going to die,
really. Except without all the embarrassment of having to
believe in God.

LIAM: No, it's nothing like that.

JEN: Jesus.

LIAM: It just means you, accept that you're dying. You accept, the life you got, was what you got, and you stop wishing there was more. You're just grateful for what there was. There's not a trick. It's just literally, accepting. And stopping fighting. And stopping struggling. And when you stop struggling, you can find a bit of peace. *(Beat.)* My mum never got to there. Because of me. Because she knew she was leaving me, with no-one. So she kept fighting, right to the end.

JEN: That's something isn't it? To never give up?

LIAM: She hated herself for dying. D'you see? Her last seconds. There was no peace. No calm. None of that for her. Just – despair. Because of me. Because she was leaving me behind. *(Beat.)* So you see I've been loved. I know what it is. And you –

He breaks off.

After a little while.

JEN: I think, if I was her –

JEN comes to a stop.

LIAM: What?

JEN doesn't know what to say.

LIAM: See? Nothing. You haven't got a clue.

JEN gets up, goes to LIAM's bedroom door.

Stops.

JEN: Maybe, you could just come give me a cwtch before you go to sleep.

LIAM: Don't think I need one, thanks.

JEN: No. But I do.

She goes.

LIAM sits there for a bit. He's thinking about following her in.

A tension drops away from him as he gives up on that thought.

He sits, shifts a few times.

RICK comes in.

RICK: 'Right.

RICK heads into the kitchen.

LIAM sits.

RICK comes back, with a pint glass of water.

Sips from it, looking at LIAM.

LIAM looks round.

LIAM: What?

RICK: Nervous?

LIAM: No.

RICK: You weren't nervous, you'd be in there already.

RICK sips again. Smiles.

RICK: Well this is one thing I can't do for you. Not that I'd mind... Goodnight, and God bless.

RICK makes to go.

LIAM: Rick.

RICK stops.

RICK: What?

LIAM looks at him.

RICK: There's no shame coming to your old man for help. If that's what you're doing.

LIAM: Forget it...

RICK: You don't want my advice?

RICK watches him a moment.

LIAM: Please.

A victory. RICK moves closer to him.

RICK: How can you be nervous going in there? How can you be nervous, climbing in that bed? It's your room. You go in there every night. It's your bed. You get in it every night.

LIAM: Except tonight now she's in it too.

RICK: That's where she's put herself. Your bed. Your room. Poor fucking girl, she couldn't be making it any fucking clearer – and here you are, fiddling with yourself on the fucking settee!

LIAM: It's not as easy as that, alright?

RICK: You know they say girls like bastards. You think that's right?

LIAM: Obviously it's a ridiculous stereotype.

RICK: Well, course.

LIAM: But having said that… it does seem…

RICK: Like girls like bastards.

LIAM: Yeah.

RICK: No they fucking don't. What a fucking stupid thing to say. Who likes a bastard? A bastard's a cunt, who wants a cunt in their lives?

LIAM: Very damaged people, with self-esteem / issues?

RICK: *(Cutting in.)* So why do girls go out with bastards? Cos no one wants to have to do everything themselves. No one wants to make all the running. You look at Jen. Don't you think she's nervous? Course she fuckin is. And every minute you don't go in there, she's wondering what the fuck is wrong with you. Or what the fuck is wrong with her. And if she was with some bastard – he'd be in there like a shot. Wouldn't he?

LIAM: Yes.

RICK: Yes he fucking would. And she would be glad, he had the fuckin balls to do that. And you think Suze. You think she likes, the way I am?

LIAM: Dunno.

RICK: Lot of the time she fuckin doesn't. But that bloke felt her up in the York and I wanted to break his face and I fuckin did it. And Suze was fuckin glad. And you.

LIAM: What about me?

RICK: You wanted me to stop drinking and you told me I had to do it and fuck me if I didn't.

LIAM: It's not the same though, is it –

RICK: And I did what you said. And I was glad you said it.

They look at each other.

RICK: She is offering herself to you. So get in there. Do what you want to. And make her yours.

RICK puts down his glass, goes.

LIAM left alone.

He thinks about it.

Isn't sure.

Then gets up.

Goes to the door.

Hesitates.

LIAM: *(Quietly.)* Fuck…

Heads back towards the sofa.

Stops. Comes back to the door.

Breathes.

Raises his hand, forms a fist to knock on the door.

Stops. Lowers his hand.

Breathes.

Opens the door and goes in.

SCENE SIX

Next morning.

LIAM enters from the kitchen, in T-shirt and pants, balancing two mugs and a plate of toast.

He thinks about trying to open the bedroom door with his hands full. Thinks better of it. Goes to the table to put down the mugs and plate.

JEN enters from the bedroom. Fully dressed.

LIAM: I couldn't remember if you said sugar or no sugar, so I guessed no sugar.

JEN: It was sugar. Two.

LIAM: See I thought – girls don't really, do they, sugar. Never mind, I'll get you another.

JEN: Don't worry about it.

LIAM: Take me two secs.

JEN: Nah my mum's coming now to pick me up.

LIAM: Yeah?

JEN: Just phoned.

LIAM: Oh okay. *(Beat.)* Didn't think you were heading straight off.

JEN: Yeah think so.

A little silence. LIAM drinks some tea.

LIAM: Was it… alright?

JEN: Alright?

LIAM: Last night. I haven't got much to compare it to.

JEN: What and I have?

LIAM: Well you know with Jordan.

She doesn't answer.

LIAM: Jen?

JEN: It was fine.

LIAM: Fine? Okay. I get the message. Not so great.

LIAM watches her.

LIAM: You want this toast?

JEN shakes her head.

LIAM: Mind if I do?

He eats.

LIAM: Bit quiet.

JEN: Bit of a hangover I think.

LIAM: You didn't have much.

JEN: You know how it gets you sometimes.

LIAM: Yeah sure.

He hesitates, then –

LIAM: Fuck was it that bad? Have I just blown it by being completely shit?

JEN: No...

LIAM: Can you just not imagine a relationship with someone who's so epically bad at shagging? I will get better, I promise. With a bit of practise.

JEN: Yeah, I'm sure you will.

LIAM: We could even... practise now a bit, if you want?

JEN: Nah I don't think so.

LIAM: No that's fine.

JEN: My mum'll be here soon, anyway.

LIAM: Yeah sure.

He stops.

LIAM: Jen?

She says nothing.

LIAM: What?

She looks at him.

LIAM: Are you feeling guilty about Jordan?

JEN: No.

LIAM: No?

JEN: Yes. Yes I am, but –

LIAM: But what?

JEN: But nothing.

LIAM: Yes you are – but it's not that?

She looks at him.

LIAM: Say.

She doesn't.

LIAM: Just spit it out.

She doesn't.

LIAM: *(Her accent.)* Come on, mun.

The mimicry makes her smile, a little.

He smiles back.

JEN: It was not, what I thought was gonna happen.

LIAM: Well, if you'd told me, a week ago, you and me'd be in that bed, you know. I mean – yeah. I get what you're saying.

JEN: It was not what I planned to happen.

LIAM: Well no Christ no.

JEN: So I'm just a bit –

She dries.

LIAM: You're a bit what?

She doesn't say.

LIAM: I mean I'm a bit. I'm a bit – fucking over the moon.

Beat.

LIAM: But you're not.

She shrugs.

LIAM: Are you alright?

JEN: I'm fine.

Beat.

LIAM: When you say, it's not what you planned. So did you then, did you think I was gonna sleep on the couch?

JEN: No, I didn't want that.

LIAM: What then?

JEN: I thought you'd sneak in with me and we'd be all cwtched up together.

LIAM: Just that?

JEN: Well, kiss and a cuddle.

LIAM: Well we had, a kiss and a cuddle.

JEN: And then… more.

LIAM: Yes.

JEN: And that… wasn't what I thought we'd do.

LIAM: Yeah cos I felt, when we were all curled up, I felt, you, grinding, just a little bit, against my leg.

JEN looks at him.

LIAM: But you didn't want – you weren't up for it?

JEN: Course, yeah, I *wanted* it.

LIAM: So what then?

JEN: I thought – we'd be all curled up together. And wanting it. But not doing it. Till it was the right time. Till I'd finished with Jordan properly and we… *(Stops.)* I thought we'd do it, I didn't think we'd do it then. But it's fine.

LIAM: How's it fine? It is not fine. What the fuck are you saying, Jen?

JEN: I've said.

LIAM: What've you said.

JEN: I just said. I just said – it isn't what I thought we'd do.

He takes a while to get to his next thought.

LIAM: Are you saying, you didn't want, what we did?

She doesn't answer.

LIAM: Jen.

JEN: I'm saying… I didn't think we'd do it, last night.

LIAM: And when you realised we *were* doing it. I didn't notice you saying stop.

JEN: I didn't want to spoil things.

LIAM: I'm sorry?

JEN: Cos we were having a lovely night. And we were. We really – we were.

LIAM: So you're saying – sorry – you're saying, you didn't want, what we did, last night.

JEN: I'm saying, it's alright.

LIAM: If you didn't want it you should've stopped me.

JEN: Well, yeah probably. But – it doesn't –

She hesitates.

JEN: Yeah okay probably I should. Sorry.

LIAM: Yeah you should. Jesus…

JEN: …I did say no.

LIAM: You did not.

JEN: I did.

LIAM: When?

She looks at him.

LIAM: At what point, exactly, did you say no?

JEN: When you were taking my knickers down.

LIAM: Well I didn't hear you.

JEN: I said it, twice.

LIAM: I didn't – really? – cos I didn't hear *anything* like that.

JEN: Are you saying I'm lying?

LIAM: No. But maybe…

JEN: What?

LIAM: Maybe, you thought you said it. But you actually /
   didn't.

JEN: *(Cutting in.)* I said it, alright –

LIAM: Not very loud.

JEN: I said it twice. I said no. Then I said no, stop.

LIAM: And when I didn't stop you should have maybe said it
   again. And maybe a bit louder?

JEN: I didn't want to make it a whole big thing.

LIAM: It wouldn't've been.

JEN: If I'd tried to stop you? You'd've just tucked yourself
   away? Been alright with that would you?

LIAM: Yes!

JEN: Wouldn't've got all moody and called me a cunt and
   Christ knows what?

LIAM: Not a chance.

JEN: Say that now…

LIAM: I'd say that always!

   She looks at him.

JEN: Thing is I think you did hear me. I thought you heard
   me. Like maybe you stopped what you were doing, just a
   second – and then you carried on. I said no, and I was sure
   you heard me say no. But you still carried on. So then I
   said no, stop. And you *still* carried on. And then I thought,
   well first I said no and then I said no, *stop*, and he's still
   carrying on so what now, what if I try and stand up to him
   then maybe it just gets much fucking worse – but it was just
   a misunderstanding. If you really didn't hear. So let's leave
   it / at that shall we?

LIAM: *(Cutting in.)* Hold on hold on hold on. You let me do it
   to you, cos you thought I'd – what? Hit you, if you didn't?

JEN: I dunno.

LIAM: You do! Course you fucking do! You know I'm not like
   that!

107

JEN: How do I know? All I know is I said stop, and you carried on.

LIAM: Oh come on, that is... how can you even say, I'm like that?

JEN: I don't know what you're like. Until you show me.

LIAM can't answer.

JEN: I didn't mind, alright. It wasn't / what I wanted

LIAM: You didn't *mind?*

JEN: But that's what you did, that's what happened, so let's just leave it be.

He looks at her.

LIAM: Would you have done that with Jordan? Gone to bed with him, wrapped yourself round him, and thought that's all it would be?

JEN: No chance.

LIAM: But you did with me.

JEN: Yeah.

LIAM: Cos I'm safe?

JEN: I thought you were, yeah.

LIAM takes this in.

LIAM: Have I done something horrible to you?

JEN: D'you feel like you have?

LIAM: Because I never –

JEN: Well then just leave it.

LIAM: Leave it how?

JEN: Chalk it up to experience.

They look at each other.

LIAM: Okay.

JEN: And just be a bit more careful next time.

LIAM: Okay yeah.

JEN: Just be a bit more fuckin respectful, alright?

LIAM: Yeah alright.

JEN: Okay. Good. There's enough pricks in the world, we don't need you turning into one.

LIAM: 'Kay.

JEN: And it would –

She hesitates.

LIAM: What?

JEN: It would mean a lot to me, if you would say you're sorry, for what you did.

He looks at her.

JEN: Cos if I knew you didn't mean, to do that, then it'd make me feel not so bad about it.

LIAM: What did I do?

JEN doesn't answer.

LIAM: What did I do?

Not immediately.

JEN: Please just tell me you didn't mean to.

LIAM looks at her.

LIAM: D'you know what I think? I think you wanted me to fuck you. So you climbed into my bed, and let me fuck you. And now you feel like a slag. And why is that, d'you think?

Not immediately –

JEN: D'you know, yeah you have done something horrible to me. And that was it, just there. *(Beat.)* I'm gonna go wait on the street.

She moves.

LIAM: Look, Jen –

She stops. Waits for him to continue.

He doesn't.

She goes.

LIAM left alone.

SCENE SEVEN

LIAM sitting.

RICK and SUZE enter.

RICK: Lemme see.

LIAM gets out his phone, swipes through a few screens. Hands it to RICK.

RICK reads, scrolls, reads some more.

RICK: Not good.

RICK gives the phone to SUZE.

She reads.

SUZE: Is this right?

LIAM: No.

SUZE: Liam…

LIAM: Not at all. No way. You know, she was here. Just then… the next morning. She started saying all this stuff.

SUZE puts the phone down.

SUZE: You stupid, stupid little / shit –

RICK: Oi.

SUZE looks at him.

RICK: Not helping. *(To LIAM.)* You heard from her since?

LIAM: No. But her mate text me, saying, she's gonna go to the police.

RICK looks at him.

SUZE: Did you?

LIAM: Did I what?

SUZE: Force her?

LIAM: Course I didn't!

SUZE looks at him.

LIAM: You're seriously asking me? *Me?*

RICK: This is all her mum. You know her mum?

LIAM shakes his head.

RICK: She sees this Jordan bloke Jen's with now. He's signed with the Ospreys hasn't he?

LIAM: I mean... I think.

RICK: You know how much they earn? Top players like?

LIAM: Not a fucking clue.

RICK: She's looking at him, you know what she's seeing? Dollar signs.

He looks at LIAM.

LIAM: You think she will go to the police?

RICK: You come between her mum, and a bunch of posh hand bags? Absolutely no doubt.

LIAM: Jesus Christ...

SUZE: Vile.

RICK: What?

SUZE: Fuckin hand bags?

RICK: You know what she's like.

SUZE: This is serious.

They look at each other. SUZE turns on LIAM.

SUZE: How could you be such a fucking little prick?

LIAM: I didn't do – it wasn't like she's saying.

SUZE: Did you, make her.

LIAM: Absolutely not, no way, not at all.

SUZE stares him out.

LIAM: She let me.

SUZE: She let you?

LIAM: Well like I was doing things and she –

RICK: She let you.

LIAM: Yes…

SUZE: Did she tell you to stop?

LIAM: No!

SUZE: Not, at all.

LIAM doesn't answer.

SUZE: Lee…

LIAM: Well she says *now* she told me to stop. But she never.

SUZE: And you're sure.

LIAM: Not even – no. I swear.

SUZE looks at him.

SUZE: Alright. Alright. *(Gathers herself.)* I knew there was something about her, little tart.

LIAM: I think she's just / confused –

SUZE: Fuck that! You are too fuckin soft you are…

RICK: I tell you what though. Cos sometimes… a girl will say no. And it's just, a thing to say. And you think, well, if she means it, she'll say it again. So you carry on. You know – just to see whether she means it, or not. And maybe she says it again. And you think, well. If she *really* means it, she'll stop me. So you carry on. Just to see.

RICK's looking at LIAM.

RICK: Maybe it was a bit like that.

LIAM: No.

RICK: They say no, cos they have to, but they don't do fuck all to stop you. They say no – but then they let you. And letting you, is saying yes. Isn't it.

LIAM doesn't answer.

RICK: Isn't it.

SUZE: Liam?

LIAM nods.

SUZE: What?

LIAM: And we curled up, went to sleep, next morning – she said it was fine, you know? Not what she planned, yeah she said that, not what she planned – but it was *fine*. And she –

He stops.

LIAM: How is she saying no, if she lets me?

RICK: She's not. She's fucking not.

SUZE: She's saying no, when she says no.

LIAM: She gets in my bed, kisses me, gets me going, and she's like, she's gagging to do it – and then she can just say no, after all that?

SUZE: Yeah.

LIAM: How is that fair?

SUZE: Say it's you buying one of your dolls. And you're in the shop. You pick the one you want. You're at the till. You've got your tenner in your hand, like you're gagging to buy it. And right there, last second, you decide you don't want to – but the bloke snatches the tenner off you. Has he stolen from you, or has he not?

LIAM says nothing.

SUZE: You fuckin know he has.

LIAM: But why wouldn't she just *stop me*?

SUZE: Cos she's scared!

LIAM: Of me? Me? I'd never – I'm not like that. *(To RICK.)* Am I?

RICK: Say she does go to the police. Say the police bring you in. Just a few questions like. You know what they'll be thinking? They'll be thinking, their daughters. And fair play to them. And I gotta say, even talking to me now, you look nervous as fuck.

LIAM: Course I'm nervous!

RICK: Why'd you be nervous, if you haven't done nothing?

LIAM: What's gonna happen to me?

RICK: Well you say to the police, what you said to me now – and they are gonna fucking go for you. And you will not come back from it.

LIAM: Aw Jesus Christ...

SUZE: Yeah pity you weren't thinking about that a bit more when you had your dick in your hand.

RICK: And you had it all planned. A-levels, university...

LIAM: What'm I gonna do?

RICK looks at him.

LIAM: What am I going to do?

RICK: Get used to having a very different kind of life to what you thought.

LIAM: I thought she liked me.

RICK: She did. A bit. She liked hanging round you. She liked knowing you wanted her. Got off on that, didn't she. And fair play. Who wouldn't. And then you put one foot wrong. And where d'you end up? I'll tell you. You'll end up hanging off the end of your belt, son.

LIAM takes this in.

SUZE: Vile...

RICK: What, you think that's wrong? You think he could take prison? Are you fucking shitting me? *(To LIAM.)* D'you think you can take it?

LIAM: No.

RICK: No. Not a chance. Not for a second. So this is it for you. This is the end. Now tell me – look at me. Fucking look at me boy.

LIAM looks at him.

RICK: This is the rest of your life, gone. Even if you get through prison, you're on some register. And everyone you ever meet. Every job. Every girl. All they gotta do is put your name in their phone – and they know. Do you deserve that? For one mistake?

RICK pauses.

RICK: Cos this is all me this is.

LIAM: This is you how?

RICK: This is me, telling you – go and take what you want. All my fault.

LIAM doesn't know what to say.

RICK: It is, isn't it.

LIAM nods.

RICK: Say it.

LIAM: This is you.

RICK: I know.

LIAM: This is your fault, if I hadn't listened to you…

SUZE: What did you tell him, Vile?

RICK: To have a bit of fucking gumption.

LIAM: He told me, to take what I wanted.

SUZE: Jesus Christ…

RICK: I said, to take what was being offered you.

LIAM: And I that's all I *did*.

RICK: I know, I know. And everything you been through. Mum gets sick. You nurse her, alone. And then you watch her die. *(Beat.)* And then cunt like me is all you got. So is it fair, you have to take this as well?

LIAM shakes his head.

RICK: Say it.

LIAM: No it is not.

RICK: Even if you made a mistake.

LIAM: It's not fucking fair…

RICK: No. And it's my fault. I'm gonna fix it.

SUZE: What the fuck are you talking about?

LIAM: Fix it how?

RICK: I'll have a word with her.

SUZE: Vile…

LIAM: What, and she'll listen?

RICK: In the end.

LIAM: But you said her mum –

RICK: Her mum can't do nothing if Jen won't.

SUZE: Don't go making this any worse, alright.

RICK: How's it gonna be fuckin worse?

LIAM: But why would –

He stops.

LIAM: Why would Jen stop, cos you say so.

RICK: Why'd you think.

LIAM doesn't answer.

RICK: There are things I could do to her, she couldn't live with.

SUZE: What the fuck are you talking about?

RICK: And I will make her understand she's safe from those things. So long as she never says another word against you.

SUZE: You're gonna threaten her? This is fuckin – come *on.*

RICK: I'm not saying it's good. I'm saying it's what's gotta be.

SUZE: It's fuckin evil.

RICK: *(To LIAM.)* Do you want me to stop her?

SUZE: *(To LIAM.)* You can't do this. You've been stupid, you've been a fucking prick but this is –

RICK: Liam.

SUZE: Alright. Alright. Just think. Say she goes to the police. She came here, she had a few drinks, she got in your bed

116

– the police aren't gonna do a thing, are they? Nothing's gonna happen to you. So just – ride it out. I'll come with you. I'll be there. I'll hold your hand –

RICK: How will you hold his hand when he's in a cell?

SUZE: *(To LIAM.)* That is not gonna happen, I swear.

RICK: Course it is.

SUZE: Cos you can make a mistake. You can do something stupid. But this isn't a mistake. This is you doing this on purpose.

RICK: Do you know what happens to kids like him inside?

She steps towards LIAM.

SUZE: Come with me. Come with me now.

LIAM: I dunno…

SUZE: It'll be alright, I swear, we'll just face it, and get through it –

RICK shoves her back.

RICK: Get the fuck away from him.

She stumbles, hurts herself a bit.

SUZE: You bastard…

RICK: You fuckin say one more word and I will end you. He goes inside, he'll end up hanging from his sheets. And that's what you're saying. You're saying, my boy, can die, cos of some fuckin slag.

He picks up SUZE's bag – throws it at her.

RICK: Get the fuck out. And you never come back here again.

She goes to leave. Stops at the door.

SUZE: Liam.

He looks away from her.

SUZE: It won't work. She's a tough little thing, you threaten her it'll just make it worse –

RICK moves fast to the door. He stops, hand raised to strike.

SUZE, scared, but stares him out.

SUZE: Fuck you. Fuck the both of you.

SUZE goes.

RICK stands a second. Then goes to where he found the secret six-pack of cans in scene four, pulls out a new can. Takes a big drink.

He turns to LIAM. Looks at him.

RICK: Is this what you want?

LIAM doesn't respond.

RICK: Is this what you want me to do? You want me to stop her.

LIAM doesn't respond.

RICK: I am not doing this, unless you say. Is this, what you want me to do?

LIAM looks at him: nods.

RICK: Say it.

LIAM: Yes.

RICK: Alright.

LIAM: Say you threaten her. And it doesn't work. And she goes to the police. Will you really hurt her?

RICK puts down his can.

RICK: Why the fuck would you even ask me that?

LIAM begins to crack. RICK moves towards him. LIAM doesn't move away.

RICK throws his arms round his son.

RICK: It's alright. It's alright, son.

Kisses his head.

RICK: Daddy's got you.

The End.

by the same author

A Soldier in Every Son –
The Rise of the Aztecs
Luis Mario Moncada
translated by Gary Owen
9781849434706

Perfect Match
9781783190607

Mrs Reynolds and the Ruffian
9781849430654

Blackthorn / In the Pipeline
9781849430708

Love Steals Us From Loneliness
9781849430548

Iphigenia in Splott
9781783198917

WWW.OBERONBOOKS.COM

Follow us on www.twitter.com/@oberonbooks
& www.facebook.com/OberonBooksLondon